ASIA

MALCOLM PORTER and KEITH LYE

CHERRYTREE BOOKS

A Cherrytree Book

Designed and produced by
A S Publishing
Text by Keith Lye
Illustrated by Malcolm Porter and Raymond Turvey

New edition published 2008 by
Cherrytree Books, part of the
Evans Publishing Group
2a Portman Mansions
Chiltern Street
London W1U 6NR

Copyright © Malcolm Porter & A S Publishing

British Library Cataloguing in Publication Data

Porter, Malcolm
    Asia. - (Continents in close-up)
    1.Children's atlases
    2.Asia - Maps for children
    I.Title II.Lye, Keith
    912.5

ISBN 9781842344613

Printed in Spain by Grafo SA

CONTINENTS IN CLOSE-UP
ASIA

This illustrated atlas combines maps, pictures, flags, globes,
information panels, diagrams and charts to give an overview
of the whole continent and a closer look at each of its countries.

COUNTRY CLOSE-UPS

Each double-page spread has these
features:

Introduction The author introduces the
most important facts about the country or
region.

Globe A globe on which you can see the
country's or region's position in the
continent and the world.

Flags Every country's flag is shown.

Information panels Every country has an
information panel which gives its area,
population and capital, and where possible
its main towns, languages, religions,
government and currency.

Pictures Important features of each
country are illustrated and captioned to
give a flavour of the country. You can find
out about physical features, famous
people, ordinary people, animals, plants,
places, products and much more.

Maps Every country is shown on a clear,
accurate map. To get the most from the
maps it helps to know the symbols which
are shown in the key on the opposite
page.

Land You can see by the colouring on
the map where the land is forested, frozen
or desert.

Height Relief hill shading shows where
the mountain ranges are. Individual
mountains are marked by a triangle.

Direction All of the maps are drawn with
north at the top of the page.

Scale All of the maps are drawn to scale
so that you can find the distance between
places in miles or kilometres.

0	200 miles
0	200 kilometres

KEY TO MAPS

INDIA	Country name
Kashmir	Region
～～～	Country border
■	More than 1 million people*
●	More than 500,000 people
•	Less than 500,000 people
□	Country capital

Hindu Kush	Mountain range
▲ Everest 8848m	Mountain with its height
∴ *Petra*	Archaeological site

Mekon	River
	Canal
	Lake
	Dam
	Island

	Forest
	Crops
	Dry grassland
	Desert
	Tundra
	Polar

Population figures in all cases are estimates, based on the most recent censuses where available or a variety of other sources.

CONTINENT CLOSE-UPS

People and Beliefs Map of population densities; chart of percentage of population by country; chart of areas of countries; map and chart of religions.

Climate and Vegetation Map of vegetation from forests to deserts; chart of land use; maps of summer and winter temperatures; map of annual rainfall.

Ecology and Environment Map of environmental damage to land and sea; panels on damaging the environment, natural hazards and endangered species; map of natural hazards.

Economy Map of agricultural and industrial products; pie-chart of gross domestic product for individual countries; panel on per capita gross domestic products; map of sources of energy.

Politics and History Map of great Asian empires; panel on great events; timeline of important dates; map of important events.

Index All the names on the maps and in the picture captions can be found in the index at the end of the book.

CONTENTS

ASIA 4

COUNTRY CLOSE-UPS

RUSSIA AND THE CAUCASUS 6

MEDITERRANEAN ASIA 8

ARABIAN PENINSULA 10

IRAQ, IRAN AND KUWAIT 12

CENTRAL ASIA 14

AFGHANISTAN AND PAKISTAN 16

INDIAN SUBCONTINENT 18

CHINA, MONGOLIA AND TAIWAN 20

KOREAN PENINSULA 22

JAPAN 24

BANGLADESH, MYANMAR AND THAILAND 26

CAMBODIA, LAOS AND VIETNAM 28

MALAYSIA, SINGAPORE AND BRUNEI 30

INDONESIA AND EAST TIMOR 32

PHILIPPINES 34

CONTINENT CLOSE-UPS

PEOPLE AND BELIEFS 36

CLIMATE AND VEGETATION 38

ECOLOGY AND ENVIRONMENT 40

ECONOMY 42

POLITICS AND HISTORY 44

INDEX 46

Giant panda
see page 20

ASIA

Asia is the largest of the continents, covering about three-tenths of the world's land area. It has more people than any other continent, with about three-fifths of the world's total population. Stretching from the icy Arctic in the north to the hot and steamy equatorial lands in the south, Asia contains huge empty deserts, as well as many of the world's highest mountains and longest rivers.

A long, mainly land border in the west separates Europe from Asia. This boundary runs north-south down the Ural Mountains in Russia, along the Ural River to the Caspian Sea and then through the Caucasus Mountains to the Black Sea. About three-quarters of Russia lies in Asia, while the rest is in Europe. Small parts of four other Asian countries also lie in Europe.

Cuneiform was an early form of writing. The wedge-shaped inscriptions were used around 5,000 years ago by the ancient Sumerian people, who founded a great civilization in the Tigris-Euphrates region in what is now Iraq. Several major civilizations developed in Asia.

Religions Asia was the home of all of the world's eight major religions. Hinduism is an ancient religion of India, as also is Buddhism, which was founded about 2,500 years ago. Judaism, Christianity and Islam developed in southwest Asia. Confucianism and Taoism were originally founded in China, while Shinto is a Japanese religion.

Rice is the chief food crop in the hot and rainy parts of Asia. The world's top eight rice producers are in Asia. In order of importance, they are China, India, Indonesia, Bangladesh, Vietnam, Thailand, Myanmar (Burma) and the Philippines.

ASIA
Area: 44,709,500sq km (17,262,400sq miles)
Population: 3,975,000,000
Number of independent countries: 49
(including Russia, Azerbaijan, Georgia, Kazakhstan and Turkey, which lie mostly in Asia)

Tigers live mainly in southern and southeastern Asia, but because of hunting and the destruction of the habitats where they once roamed free, they are an endangered species. Poachers kill tigers for their skins, bones and other body parts which are used to make potions in parts of Asia.

Great Wall of China This is the longest structure ever built. It is about 7,400 km (4,600 miles) long. Construction probably began in the 5th century BC and continued until the 17th century AD. The wall protected China from invaders from the north.

Poverty is widespread in Asia. Most countries depend on farming, but some have grown rich through manufacturing and trade. The Petronas Towers in Kuala Lumpur, Malaysia, are a symbol of Southeast Asia's increasing prosperity.

5

RUSSIA AND THE CAUCASUS

Russia is the world's largest country. About three-quarters of it lies in Asia, east of the Ural Mountains and the Caspian Sea. The rest is in Europe. From 1922 Russia was the centre of the Communist USSR (Union of Soviet Socialist Republics), known as the Soviet Union. In 1991 the Soviet Union split up into 15 countries.

Three of these countries – Armenia, Azerbaijan and Georgia – border Russia in the southwest. Together they are called Transcaucasia after the high Caucasus Mountains that lie to the north. Conflict has occurred in Chechnya, Russia, and also in parts of Transcaucasia, as rival ethnic and religious groups have fought for independence.

Woolly mammoths lived during the Ice Age in Siberia (a name often used for Asian Russia). They died out about 10,000 years ago, but bodies of mammoths have been found perfectly preserved in the frozen subsoil of Siberia.

Oil and natural gas are abundant in Russia, and the country is a major producer. Azerbaijan also has large oil deposits in the Caspian Sea. Russia has most of the minerals it needs, including bauxite, copper, diamonds, iron ore, nickel and phosphates (used to make fertilizers).

RUSSIA

Area: 17,075,400sq km (6,592,850sq miles), of which about 75% is in Asia
Highest point: Mount Elbrus, in the Caucasus Mountains, 5,642m (18,510ft)
Population: 142,894,000 (about 20% of whom live in Asian Russia)
Capital and largest city: Moscow (pop 10,469,000)
Other large cities (in Asian Russia):
Novosibirsk (1,426,000)
Yekaterinburg (1,290,000)
Omsk (1,130,000)
Chelyabinsk (1,058,000)
Krasnoyarsk (907,000)
Irkutsk (584,000)
Official language: Russian
Religions: Christianity (Russian Orthodox 20%), Islam 10%
Government: Republic
Currency: Rouble

GEORGIA

Area: 69,700sq km (26,911sq miles), 21% of which is in Europe
Highest point: Mt Shkhara 5,201m (17,163ft)
Population: 4,661,000
Capital: Tbilisi (pop 1,064,000)
Official language: Georgian
Religions: Christianity (84%), Islam (10%)
Government: Republic
Currency: Lari

ARMENIA

Area: 29,800sq km (11,506sq miles)
Highest point: Mt Aragats 4,090m (13,419ft)
Population: 2,976,000
Capital: Yerevan (pop 1,079,000)
Official language: Armenian
Religions: Christianity (Armenian Apostolic 95%, other Christian 4%)
Government: Republic
Currency: Dram

AZERBAIJAN

Area: 86,600sq km (33,436sq miles), 17% of which is in Europe
Highest point: Bazar Dyuzi 4,466m (14,652ft)
Population: 7,962,000
Capital: Baku (pop 1,816,000)
Official language: Azerbaijani
Religion: Islam (93%)
Government: Republic
Currency: Manat

Black Sea

Elbrus 5642m

GEORGIA

Shkhara 5201m

Aragats 4090m

Tbilisi

Caspian Sea

Yerevan

Bazar Dyuzi 4466m

ARMENIA

AZERBAIJAN

Baku

Ural Mountains

Ob

West S

Ural

Yekaterinburg

Chelyabinsk

Irty

Kurgan

Orsk

Su

Om

Joseph Stalin (1879-1953) was born in Georgia. He played a leading part in the 1917 Russian Revolution, which turned Russia into a Communist country. From 1929 until his death in 1953, Stalin was the dictator of the Soviet Union. His rule was marked by great brutality.

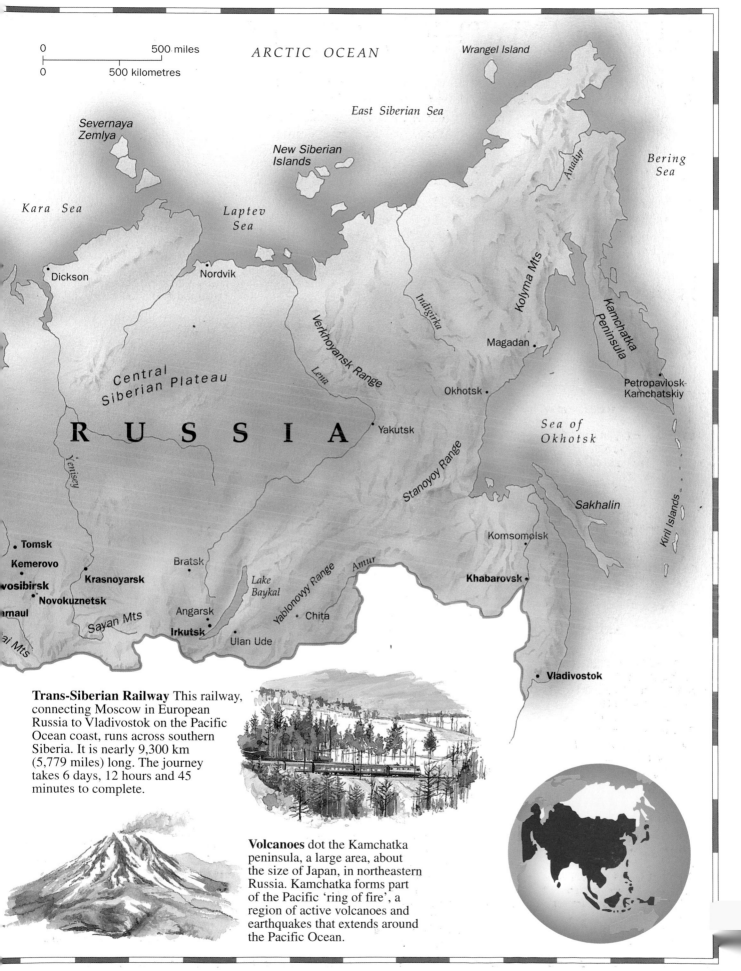

0   500 miles

0   500 kilometres

ARCTIC OCEAN

Wrangel Island

East Siberian Sea

Severnaya Zemlya

New Siberian Islands

Bering Sea

Kara Sea

Laptev Sea

Dickson

Nordvik

Kolyma Mts

Indigirka

Kamchatka Peninsula

Magadan

Verkhoyansk Range

Central Siberian Plateau

Lena

R U S S I A

Okhotsk

Petropavlosk-Kamchatskiy

Yakutsk

Sea of Okhotsk

Yenisey

Stanoyoy Range

Sakhalin

Komsomolsk

Kuril Islands

Tomsk

Bratsk

Kemerovo

Lake Baykal

Khabarovsk

vosibirsk

Krasnoyarsk

Novokuznetsk

Yablonovyy Range

Amur

rnaul

Angarsk

Chita

Sayan Mts

Irkutsk

Ulan Ude

ai Mts

Vladivostok

Trans-Siberian Railway This railway, connecting Moscow in European Russia to Vladivostok on the Pacific Ocean coast, runs across southern Siberia. It is nearly 9,300 km (5,779 miles) long. The journey takes 6 days, 12 hours and 45 minutes to complete.

Volcanoes dot the Kamchatka peninsula, a large area, about the size of Japan, in northeastern Russia. Kamchatka forms part of the Pacific 'ring of fire', a region of active volcanoes and earthquakes that extends around the Pacific Ocean.

MEDITERRANEAN ASIA

At the eastern end of the Mediterranean Sea lies a group of six Asian countries. The largest is Turkey, a small part of which lies in Europe, west of the waterway linking the Mediterranean and Black seas. Turkey is a largely mountainous country with a mild, rainy climate. Cyprus and Lebanon have pleasant sunny climates, but hot deserts cover much of Israel, Jordan and Syria.

Israel was founded as a Jewish state in the ancient region of Palestine in 1948, but it has had to fight for its existence against its Arab neighbours in wars in 1948-9, 1956, 1967 and 1973. In 1967 it gained large areas from Egypt, Jordan and Syria.

 TURKEY

Area: 774,815sq km (299,158sq miles), 97% of which is in Asia
Highest point: Mt Ararat 5,185m (17,011ft)
Population: 70,414,000
Capital: Ankara (pop 3,428,000)
Official language: Turkish
Religion: Islam
Government: Republic
Currency: Turkish lira

 CYPRUS

Area: 9,251sq km (3,572sq miles)
Highest point: Mt Olympus 1,952m (6,403ft)
Population: 784,000
Capital: Nicosia (pop 205,000)
Official languages: Greek, Turkish
Religions: Greek Orthodox (78%), Islam (18%)
Government: Republic
Currency: Cyprus pound, Turkish new lira

 SYRIA

Area: 185,180sq km (71,498sq miles)
Highest point: Mt Hermon 2,814m (9,232ft)
Population: 18,881,000
Capital: Damascus (pop 2,228,000)
Official language: Arabic
Religion: Islam (90%)
Government: Republic
Currency: Syrian pound

 LEBANON

Area: 10,400sq km (4,015sq miles)
Highest point: Qurnat as Sawda 3,083m (10,115ft)
Population: 3,874,000
Capital: Beirut (pop 1,792,000)
Official language: Arabic
Religions: Islam (60%), Christianity (39%)
Government: Republic
Currency: Lebanese pound

Earthquakes occur in northern Turkey as the land moves along huge faults (cracks) in the earth's crust. At least 13,000 people died in 1999 when an earthquake struck the area near Izmit in northwestern Turkey.

 ISRAEL

Area: 21,056sq km (8,130sq miles)
Highest point: Mt Meron 1,208m (3,963ft)
Population: 6,352,000
Capital: Jerusalem (pop 686,000)
Official languages: Hebrew, Arabic
Religions: Judaism (80%), Islam (15%)
Government: Republic
Currency: New sheqel

 JORDAN

Area: 97,740sq km (37,738sq miles)
Highest point: Jabal Ramm 1,754m (5,755ft)
Population: 5,907,000
Capital: Amman (pop 1,237,000)
Official language: Arabic
Religions: Islam (94%), Christianity (6%)
Government: Monarchy
Currency: Jordan dinar

Jerusalem is a holy city for Christians, Jews and Muslims. From 1949, Israel controlled western Jerusalem and made it their capital in 1950. Eastern Jerusalem was held by Lebanon until Israeli forces captured eastern Jerusalem during the 1967 Arab-Israeli War. Here devout Jews pray at the Wailing Wall, a sacred place of Judaism.

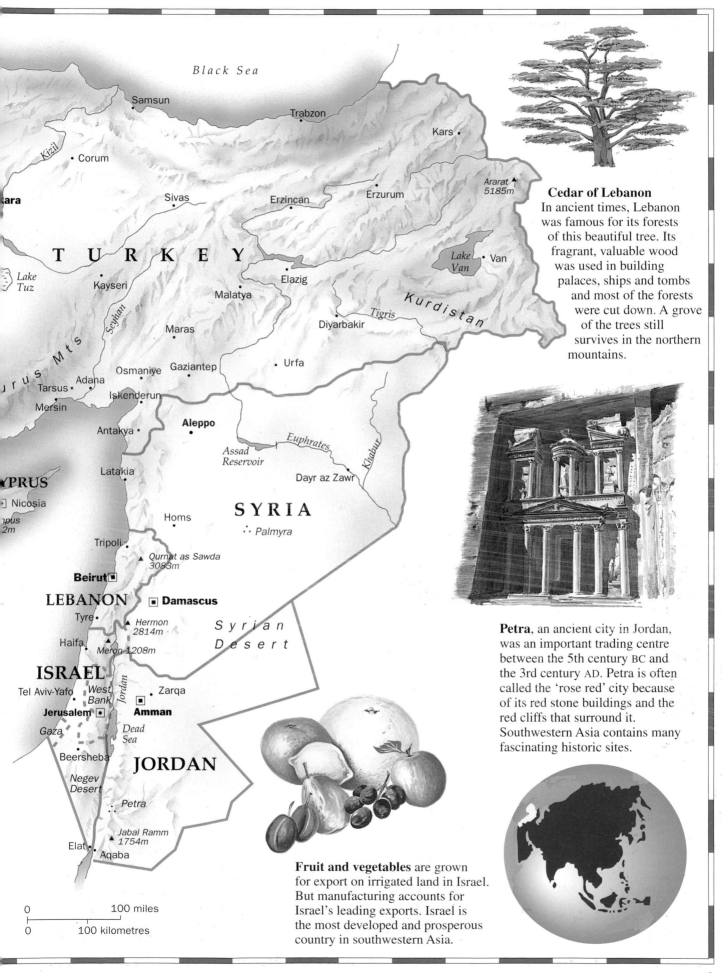

Black Sea

Samsun

Trabzon

Kars •

Corum •

Kizil

Ararat ▲
5185m

ara

Sivas

Erzincan

Erzurum

*Lake
Van* • Van

Kayseri

Malatya

Elazig

*Lake
Tuz*

K u r d i s t a n

Maras

Diyarbakir

Tigris

T U R K E Y

urus Mts

Osmaniye Gaziantep

• Urfa

Adana

Tarsus •

Iskenderun

Mersin •

Antakya •

Aleppo

Euphrates

Khabur

*Assad
Reservoir*

Latakia •

• Dayr az Zawr

PRUS

pus
2m

Nicosia

Tripoli •

Homs •

S Y R I A

∴ *Palmyra*

▲ *Qurnat as Sawda
3083m*

Beirut ▣

LEBANON

▣ **Damascus**

Tyre •

▲ *Hermon
2814m*

*S y r i a n
D e s e r t*

Haifa •

▲ *Meron 1208m*

ISRAEL

Tel Aviv-Yafo •

*West
Bank*

• Zarqa

Jordan

Jerusalem ▣

▣
Amman

Gaza

*Dead
Sea*

Beersheba •

JORDAN

*Negev
Desert*

Petra

▲ *Jabal Ramm
1754m*

Elat •

Aqaba

0	100 miles
0	100 kilometres

Cedar of Lebanon
In ancient times, Lebanon was famous for its forests of this beautiful tree. Its fragrant, valuable wood was used in building palaces, ships and tombs and most of the forests were cut down. A grove of the trees still survives in the northern mountains.

Petra, an ancient city in Jordan, was an important trading centre between the 5th century BC and the 3rd century AD. Petra is often called the 'rose red' city because of its red stone buildings and the red cliffs that surround it. Southwestern Asia contains many fascinating historic sites.

Fruit and vegetables are grown for export on irrigated land in Israel. But manufacturing accounts for Israel's leading exports. Israel is the most developed and prosperous country in southwestern Asia.

ARABIAN PENINSULA

The Arabian peninsula lies between the Red Sea and The Gulf (also known as the Arabian or Persian Gulf). Hot, thinly populated deserts cover most of the peninsula. Farming is possible only around oases where people can get water from underground rocks. But Bahrain, Oman, Qatar, Saudi Arabia and United Arab Emirates all have rich oil reserves. Yemen is the poorest country in this region.

Mecca in Saudi Arabia was the birthplace of the Prophet Mohammed (?AD 570-632), who founded the religion of Islam. Every year more than a million Muslims from all over the world visit Mecca on a pilgrimage called the hajj.

SAUDI ARABIA

Area: 2,149,690sq km (830,000sq miles)
Highest point: 3,139m (10,279ft)
Population: 27,020,000
Capital: Riyadh (pop 5,126,000)
Official language: Arabic
Religion: Islam
Government: Monarchy
Currency: Saudi riyal

YEMEN

Area: 527,968sq km (203,850sq miles)
Highest point: Hadur Shuayb 3,760m (12,336ft)
Population: 21,456,000
Capital: Sana (pop 1,469,000)
Official language: Arabic
Religion: Islam
Government: Republic
Currency: Yemeni rial

OMAN

Area: 212,457sq km (82,030sq miles)
Highest point: Jabal Ash Sham 3,035m (9,957ft)
Population: 3,102,000
Capital: Muscat (pop 638,000)
Official language: Arabic
Religions: Islam (88%), Hinduism (7%)
Government: Monarchy
Currency: Omani rial

UNITED ARAB EMIRATES

Area: 83,600sq km (32,278sq miles)
Highest point: Jabal Yibir 1,527m (5,010ft)
Population: 2,603,000
Capital: Abu Dhabi (pop 475,000)
Official language: Arabic
Religion: Islam (96%)
Government: Federation of seven emirates
Currency: UAE dirham

QATAR

Area: 11,000sq km (4,247sq miles)
Population: 885,000
Capital: Doha (pop 286,000)
Official language: Arabic
Religion: Islam (95%)
Government: Monarchy
Currency: Qatar riyal

BAHRAIN

Area: 694sq km (268sq miles)
Population: 699,000
Capital: Manama (pop 139,000)
Official language: Arabic
Religions: Islam (80%), Christianity (9%)
Government: Monarchy
Currency: Bahrain dinar

Arabian oryx This graceful antelope was almost extinct in the Arabian peninsula until some were taken to Phoenix Zoo, Arizona. There, a world herd was established. Animals from this herd have been released in Jordan, Oman and Saudi Arabia.

Muslim women often follow the *hijab* dress code by wearing a simple scarf. Others cover their face with the *niqab*. This form of clothing is required by strict Muslim teachings, but women in some Muslim countries wear western dress.

Al Jawf

Tabuk

An Nafud

Al Wajh

Medina

Yanbu

Jiddah

Mecca

At Ta

Red Sea

Rub al Khali This bleak desert lies mainly in southern Saudi Arabia and also in Yemen. It is often called the 'Empty Quarter' because it contains the world's largest expanse of sand. Plants are almost non-existent, growing only at oases.

Dates are the nutritious fruits of the date palm, the commonest tree in the Arabian peninsula. The tree trunks are used in building and the leaves are used to make baskets and mats. Dates have been an important food in southwestern Asia for at least 5,000 years.

Camels can travel long distances without having to drink water. They are often called the 'ships of the desert' because they were the traditional means of transporting people and goods across deserts.

Oil tankers transport oil from the Gulf region all around the world. Saudi Arabia is the largest producer and exporter of oil and it has the world's largest known reserves. Money from oil sales has been used to develop industries and welfare services in the Arabian peninsula.

Hafar

uraydah

The Gulf

Damman

BAHRAIN
Manama

QATAR
Doha

Al Hufuf

Riyadh

Haradh

Sharjah

Dubai

Abu Dhabi

UNITED ARAB
EMIRATES

Strait of Hormuz

OMAN

*Jabal Yibir
1527m*

*Gulf of
Oman*

Al Khaburah

Muscat

*Jabal Ash Sham
3035m*

SAUDI ARABIA

Rub al Khali

(Empty Quarter)

OMAN

Al Masira

Dhufar

Arabian Sea

Hadhramaut

Salalah

Sana
Hadur Shuayb 3760m

YEMEN

Hudaydah

abid

Taiz

cha

Aden

Al Mukalla

0   200 miles

0   200 kilometres

IRAQ, IRAN AND KUWAIT

Iraq contains large deserts but also has a fertile region called Mesopotamia. Mesopotamia means 'the land between the rivers'. The rivers are the Tigris and Euphrates, which rise in Turkey and flow across Iraq. Mesopotamia was the place where Sumer, the oldest known civilization, developed. Later civilizations in Mesopotamia included those of Assyria and Babylon. Iran (formerly Persia) also has many magnificent historic sites, including the ancient city of Persepolis, which was destroyed by Alexander the Great.

Since the 1980s, these oil-rich, Muslim countries have been at war. Iran and Iraq fought between 1980 and 1988. In 1990 Iraq invaded Kuwait and an allied force led by the United States drove Iraqi troops out of Kuwait. A second invasion in 2003 deposed Iraq's dictator Saddam Hussein and elections for a new government were held in 2005. But violence continued and many Iraqis have become refugees.

IRAQ

Area: 438,317sq km (169,235sq miles)
Highest point: 3,609m (11,480ft) in Zagros Mts
Population: 26,500,000
Capital and largest city: Baghdad (pop 5,500,000)
Other large cities: Mosul, Irbil, Basra
(no reliable figures available)
Official languages: Arabic, Kurdish
Religions: Islam (97%), Christianity (3%)
Government: Republic
Currency: New Iraqi dinar

⟨۞⟩ IRAN

Area: 1,633,188sq km (642,161sq miles)
Highest point: Mt Damavand 5,604m (18,386ft)
Population: 68,688,000
Capital and largest city: Tehran (pop 7,190,000)
Other large cities: Mashhad (1,990,000)
Tabriz (1,461,000)
Esfahan (1,381,000)
Official language: Farsi (Persian)
Religion: Islam (99%)
Government: Islamic republic
Currency: Iranian rial

KUWAIT

Area: 17,818sq km (6,880sq miles)
Population: 2,418,000
Capital: Kuwait (pop 1,222,000)
Official language: Arabic
Religion: Islam (85%)
Government: Monarchy
Currency: Kuwaiti dinar

Kurds are a people who live in mountainous regions in Armenia, Iran, Iraq, Syria and Turkey. They have suffered much political repression and many Kurds want to create their own country. Following the Iraq war, the Iraqi Kurds gained political freedom and their homeland is relatively free of violence.

Ur was a city in ancient Sumer, identified in the Bible as the home of Abraham. The people of Sumer built temples that stood on the top of pyramid-like structures, called *ziggurats*.

Persian carpets are world famous for their beauty. Craft industries are important in Iran. Other products made by hand include glassware, leather, pottery and metal goods, such as trays and tea services.

0 _____ 200 miles
0 _____ 200 kilometres

Caspian Sea

Gorgan

Mashhad

urz Mts
ehran · Damavand
▪ 5604m
· Rey

Qom

Dasht-e Kavir

· Kashan

I R A N

▪ Esfahan

Yazd ·

Dasht-e Lut

Kerman ·

∴ Persepolis

Zahedan ·

· Shiraz

· Bam

ushehr

The Gulf

Bandar Abbas

Strait of Hormuz

Chah Bahar

Tehran, the capital of Iran, stands at the foot of the Elburz Mountains. This busy industrial city has universities and museums that exhibit treasures from the region's earlier civilizations. This is the Shayhad monument.

Ayatollah Khomeini (1900?-89) led the revolution in 1979 that overthrew the shah (king) of Iran and turned the country into an Islamic republic. Iran's laws are now based closely on the teachings of Islam.

Wars have raged periodically in southwestern Asia for the last 70 years. Most recently Saddam Hussein's Iraq was twice opposed by coalitions led by the United States. The Iraqi military was disbanded in 2003 though forces have been trained to support the new government.

Kuwait is an oil-rich country at the head of the Gulf. The invasion of Kuwait by Iraq in 1990 and the 1991 Gulf War caused pollution on a huge scale and great damage to Kuwait's oilfields. These were repaired at a cost of billions of dollars.

CENTRAL ASIA

The five countries of Central Asia were once part of the Soviet Union. They became independent in 1991, when the Soviet Union split up. Kazakhstan, the world's ninth largest country, lies mainly in Asia, though a small area in the west lies in Europe.

Central Asia contains mountains, deserts, huge lakes and vast grassy plains called steppes. Attempts to develop the land have created environmental problems. Much of the river water that once flowed into the Aral Sea, for example, is now used by farmers and the huge lake has shrunk. Areas that were once fishing grounds are now desert.

KAZAKHSTAN

Area: 2,717,000sq km (1,049,040sq miles), 4% of which is in Europe
Highest point: Mt Teneri 6,398m (20,991ft)
Population: 15,233,000
Capital: Astana (pop 332,000)
Official language: Kazakh
Religions: Islam (47%), Christianity (10%)
Government: Republic
Currency: Tenge

UZBEKISTAN

Area: 447,400sq km (172,742sq miles)
Highest point: 4,643m (15,233ft) in the southeast
Population: 27,307,000
Capital: Tashkent (pop 2,155,000)
Official language: Uzbek
Religion: Islam (88%)
Government: Republic
Currency: Uzbekistani som

TURKMENISTAN

Area: 488,100sq km (188,546sq miles)
Highest point: Kugitangtau 3,137m (10,292ft)
Population: 5,043,000
Capital: Ashgabat (pop 574,000)
Official language: Turkmen
Religion: Islam (89%)
Government: Republic
Currency: Manat

TAJIKISTAN

Area: 145,100sq km (56,023sq miles)
Highest point: Ismoili Somoni 7,495m (24,590ft)
Population: 7,321,000
Capital: Dushanbe (pop 554,000)
Official language: Tajik
Religion: Islam (85%)
Government: Republic
Currency: Somoni

KYRGYZSTAN

Area: 198,500sq km (76,641sq miles)
Highest point: Jengish Chokusu 7,439m (24,406ft)
Population: 5,214,000
Capital: Bishkek (pop 806,000)
Official language: Kyrgyz
Religion: Islam (75%)
Government: Republic
Currency: Kyrgyzstani som

Cotton is a major crop throughout Central Asia and agriculture is the main activity. The governments of these former Communist countries have been working since 1991 to introduce private ownership of the land and industries.

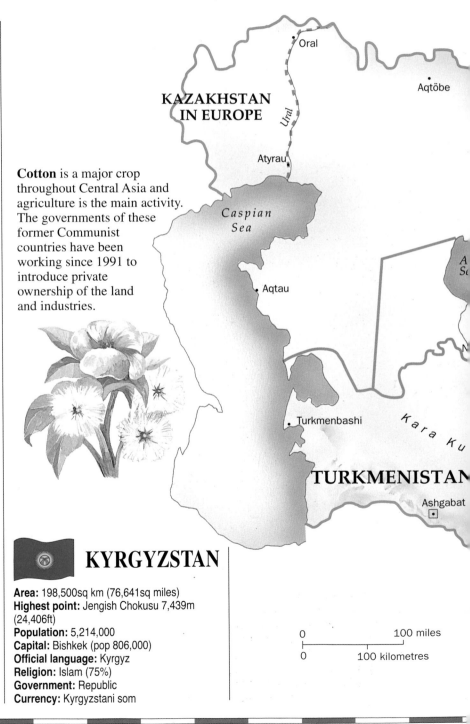

KAZAKHSTAN IN EUROPE

Oral

Aqtöbe

Ural

Atyrau

Caspian Sea

Aqtau

Turkmenbashi

Kara Ku

TURKMENISTAN

Ashgabat

A Se

0   100 miles
0   100 kilometres

Aral Sea This saltwater lake on the border between Uzbekistan and Kazakhstan has lost 75 per cent of its volume since 1960. Much of the river water that supplied it is now used to irrigate cotton fields. The local fishing industry has been destroyed, with fishing boats left high and dry.

Deserts cover much of Turkmenistan, Uzbekistan and southern Kazakhstan. Northern Kazakhstan contains high plains covered by dry grassland, or steppe. Farmers on horseback look after their cattle and sheep.

Petropavl

Qostanay

Irtysh

Pavlodar

Astana

Semey

Öskemen

Lake Zaysan

Qaraghandy

K A Z A K H S T A N

Baykonur · Zhezqazghan

Lake Balkhush

Almaty

Teneri 6398m

Jengish Chokusu 7439m

Zhambyl

Bishkek

Shymkent

KYRGYZSTAN

Syrdarya

Kyzyl Kum

Namangan

ZBEKISTAN

Tashkent

Andijon

Nawoiy

Bukhara

Samarkand

Ismoili Somoni 7495m

Amudarya

4643m

Dushanbe

TAJIKISTAN

Pamirs

Kugitangtau 3137m

Baykonur in Kazakhstan was the space centre for the former Soviet Union. Since the Soviet Union was dissolved in 1991, Russia has paid Kazakhstan for use of the site. The first manned orbital flight in 1961 was launched from Baykonur.

Samarkand, in Uzbekistan, was once the capital of the empire of the Mongol emperor Timur (or Tamerlaine). The city has beautiful mosques and other fine buildings, many decorated with mosaics. Islam is the chief religion in Central Asia.

AFGHANISTAN AND PAKISTAN

Landlocked Afghanistan is one of the world's poorest countries. Highlands and mountains cover most of the land. Afghanistan has suffered drought, famine and wars. In 1989 a Russian occupation force was ousted. By 1996 most of the country had fallen under the control of the Taleban, a strict Muslim group. In 2001 the Taleban were accused of aiding Al Qaeda terrorists, and a US-led invasion overthrew them. An elected government was set up, but fighting continued and many Afghans became refugees.

Pakistan has high mountains but also fertile plains drained by the Indus River and its tributaries. Pakistan became independent in 1947, when it broke away from British India. It remains in dispute with India over the region of Kashmir.

AFGHANISTAN

Area: 652,090sq km (251,773sq miles)
Highest point: Nowshak, in the Hindu Kush, 7,485m (24,557ft)
Population: 31,057,000
Capital and largest city: Kabul (pop 2,956,000)
Other large cities: Kandahar (401,000)
Mazar-e-Sharif (315,000)
Herat (278,000)
Jalalabad (209,000)
Official languages: Dari (Persian), Pashto
Religion: Islam
Government: Republic
Currency: Afghani

PAKISTAN

Area: 796,095sq km (307,374sq miles)
Highest point: K2 8,611m (28,250ft)
Population: 165,804,000
Capital: Islamabad (pop 698,000)
Largest cities: Karachi (10,032,000)
Lahore (5,452,000)
Faisalabad (2,582,000)
Rawalpindi (1,793,000)
Gujranwala (1,421,000)
Hyderabad (1,417,000)
Official language: Urdu
Religion: Islam (95%)
Government: Military regime
Currency: Pakistani rupee

Muslims pray five times a day, at dawn, noon, in the afternoon and evening, and finally at nightfall. When they pray, they always face Mecca, the birthplace of the Prophet Mohammed. Afghanistan and Pakistan are both Islamic states.

Fruits of many kinds are grown in Afghanistan and Pakistan. The economies of both countries depend on agriculture. Wheat is their chief food crop. Many farmers raise goats and sheep. Manufacturing is increasing in Pakistan.

Herat

Harirud

A F G H A N I S T A N

Helmand

Kandahar

Rigestan Desert

Baluchistan Plateau

Gwadar

Arabian Sea

0	100 miles
0	100 kilometres

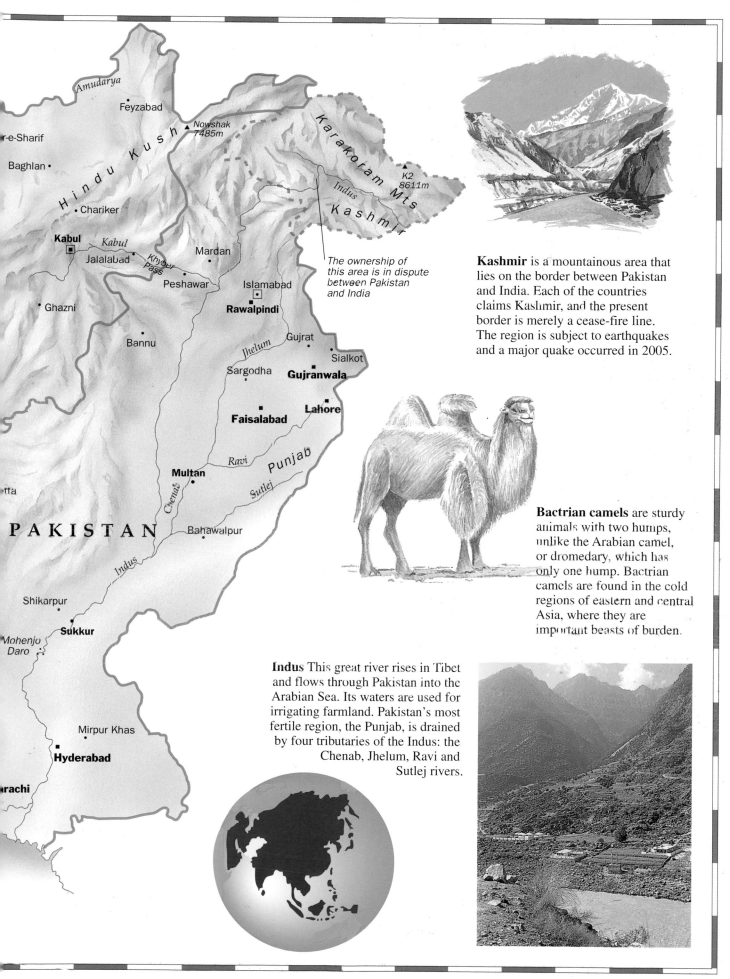

Kashmir is a mountainous area that lies on the border between Pakistan and India. Each of the countries claims Kashmir, and the present border is merely a cease-fire line. The region is subject to earthquakes and a major quake occurred in 2005.

Bactrian camels are sturdy animals with two humps, unlike the Arabian camel, or dromedary, which has only one hump. Bactrian camels are found in the cold regions of eastern and central Asia, where they are important beasts of burden.

Indus This great river rises in Tibet and flows through Pakistan into the Arabian Sea. Its waters are used for irrigating farmland. Pakistan's most fertile region, the Punjab, is drained by four tributaries of the Indus: the Chenab, Jhelum, Ravi and Sutlej rivers.

The ownership of this area is in dispute between Pakistan and India

PAKISTAN

Amudarya
Feyzabad
Nowshak 7485m
Karakoram Mts
K2 8611m
Kashmir
Hindu Kush
r-e-Sharif
Baghlan
Chariker
Kabul
Jalalabad
Khyber Pass
Peshawar
Ghazni
Mardan
Islamabad
Rawalpindi
Bannu
Jhelum
Gujrat
Sialkot
Sargodha
Gujranwala
Lahore
Faisalabad
Ravi
Punjab
Chenab
Multan
Sutlej
Bahawalpur
Indus
Shikarpur
Mohenjo Daro
Sukkur
Mirpur Khas
Hyderabad
Karachi

INDIAN SUBCONTINENT

India is the world's seventh largest country, but in population it ranks second only to China. Northern India is mountainous, and long rivers, including the Ganges, flow down from the mountains and across the fertile plains to the south of the mountains. South India is a tableland called the Deccan. India became independent from Britain in 1947.

The Indian subcontinent also includes Bhutan and Nepal, two mountainous countries in the Himalaya region, and the beautiful island country of Sri Lanka (formerly called Ceylon) which lies off the southern tip of India. The Maldives is an island nation lying to the southwest of southern India. A tsunami in 2004 struck the coasts of India, the Maldives and Sri Lanka.

 INDIA

Area: 3,287,590sq km (1,269,346sq miles)
Highest point: Kanchenjunga 8,598m (28,208ft)
Population: 1,095,352,000
Capital: New Delhi (pop 301,000)
Largest cities: Mumbai (formerly Bombay, 16,086,000)
Kolkata (Calcutta, 13,058,000)
Delhi (12,441,000)
Chennai (Madras, 6,353,000)
Official languages: Hindi, English
Religions: Hinduism (81%), Islam (13%),
Government: Federal republic
Currency: Indian rupee

 SRI LANKA

Area: 65,610sq km (25,332sq miles)
Highest point: Pidurutalagala 2,524m (8,281ft)
Population: 20,222,000
Capital: Colombo (pop 648,000)
Official languages: Sinhala, Tamil
Religions: Buddhism (69%), Hinduism (7%), Islam (7%), Christianity (6%)
Government: Republic
Currency: Sri Lankan rupee

 NEPAL

Area: 147,181sq km (56,827sq miles)
Highest point: Mt Everest 8,848m (29,029ft)
Population: 28,287,000
Capital: Kathmandu (pop 741,000)
Other large cities: Lalitpur (189,000)
Official language: Nepali
Religions: Hinduism (85%), Buddhism (11%)
Government: Monarchy
Currency: Nepalese rupee

 MALDIVES

Area: 298sq km (115sq miles)
Highest point: 24m (80ft) on Wilingili Island west of Male
Population: 359,000
Capital: Male (pop 83,000)
Official language: Dhivehi
Religion: Islam
Government: Republic
Currency: Maldivian rufiyaa

 BHUTAN

Area: 47,000sq km (18,147sq miles)
Highest point: Kula Kangri 7,554m (24,783ft)
Population: 672,000
Capital: Thimphu (pop 35,000)
Official language: Dzongkha
Religions: Buddhism (75%), Hinduism (25%)
Government: Monarchy
Currency: Ngultrum

0 _____ 200 miles
0 _____ 200 kilometres

Srinagar • Leh
• Jammu
Amritsar
• Jullundur
Ludhiana • Chandigarh
Dehra Dun
Delhi • Meerut
Bikaner • New Delhi • Aligarh • Bare
Jaipur • Luck
Agra • Kanpur
• Ajmer
Gwalior
• Jodhpur
Great Indian (Thar) Desert
• Kota

Bhopal
Ahmadabad Ujjain
Indore
Jamnagar • Rajkot • Vadodara *Narmada*
Bhavnagar • **Nagpur**
Surat
Aurangabad **I N D I A**
Arabian Sea
Mumbai *Godavari*
• Pune Wara
Sholapur
Deccan Plateau
Goa *Western Ghats* **Hyderabad**
Bangalore Ch
Mangalore •
• Mysore
Salem
Kozhikode • **Tiruchchira**
Coimbatore
Cochin • **Madurai**
Tirunelveli
Thiruvananthapuram

MALDIVES *INDIAN OCEAN*

• Male

Himalayas The Himalayas is a range of mountains that borders the Indian subcontinent in the north. It contains the world's highest peak, Mount Everest, which stands on the border between Nepal and China. Bhutan also contains part of the Himalayas.

NEPAL

Kathmandu

Everest 8848m

Kanchenjunga 8598m

Kula Kangri 7554m

BHUTAN

Thimphu

Darjiling

Lalitpur

Guwahati

Gorakhpur

Imphal

abad

Patna

Bhagalpur

bad

Ganges

Varanasi

Asanol

Ranchi

Jamshedpur

Kolkata

Haora

ilaspur

our

Cuttack

Bay of Bengal

Vishakhapatnam

awada

RI LANKA

durutalagala 524m

bo

Mohandas Gandhi (1869-1948) was a great political and spiritual leader in India. People called him the *Mahatma*, a title meaning 'Great Soul'. Gandhi helped to free India from Britain, using non-violent resistance to oppose the government. He was assassinated in 1948.

Hindu gods are believed by most Hindus to be different aspects of the one god Brahman. Statues like this one are placed in temples and homes. Hindu beliefs and practices vary throughout India and worshippers celebrate many festivals.

Taj Mahal One of the world's most famous and beautiful buildings, the Taj Mahal is in Agra, northwestern India. It was built between 1630 and 1650 by an Indian ruler, Shah Jehan, as a tomb for his beloved wife, Mumtaz Mahal.

Tea India and Sri Lanka are among the world's leading tea producers. India's chief food crops are rice and wheat. India has more cattle than any other country but Hindus do not eat meat. They regard cattle as sacred animals.

CHINA, MONGOLIA AND TAIWAN

China is the world's third largest country after Russia and Canada, but in population it ranks first. China includes Hong Kong, a former British territory that was returned to China in 1997, and Macau, a former Portuguese territory that was returned in 1999. China also claims the island of Taiwan, but the Taiwanese do not want to be ruled by the Communist government of China.

China became a Communist country in 1949, but since the late 1970s it has been changing. The government has encouraged private ownership of land and invited foreign companies to invest in new industries in eastern China. By 2006 China had the world's fourth largest economy, though millions of Chinese still live in poverty.

CHINA

Area: 9,562,074sq km (3,691,938sq miles)
Highest point: Mt Everest 8,848m (29,029ft)
Population: 1,313,974,000
Capital: Beijing (pop 10,848,000)
Other large cities: Shanghai (12,837,000)
Tianjin (9,156,000)
Shenyang (4,828,000)
Chongqing (4,635,000)
Wuhan (4,236,000)
Official language: Mandarin Chinese
Religions: Chinese folk religions (20%),
Buddhism (8%), Christianity (6%)
Government: People's republic
Currency: Yuan (Renminbi)

MONGOLIA

Area: 1,566,500sq km (604,829sq miles)
Highest point: 4,362m (14,311ft) in the Altai Mts
Population: 2,832,000
Capital: Ulan Bator (pop 812,000)
Official language: Khalkha Mongolian
Religions: Lamaism, a kind of Buddhism, (50%),
Islam (4%)
Government: Republic
Currency: Tugrik (Togrog)

TAIWAN

Area: 35,980sq km (13,892sq miles)
Highest point: Tu Shan 3,997m (13,113ft)
Population: 23,036,000
Capital: Taipei (pop 2,550,000)
Official language: Mandarin Chinese, Taiwanese
Religions: Traditional beliefs embracing
Buddhism, Confucianism and Taoism
Government: Republic
Currency: New Taiwan dollar

Giant panda This endangered animal is the symbol used by WWF (formerly World Wide Fund for Nature). In the wild, pandas are found in only a few remaining bamboo forests on mountain slopes in western and southwestern China. The giant panda is protected by law.

Mao Zedong (1893-1976) led the struggle to make China a Communist country. From 1949 he was a powerful ruler whose writings influenced many people around the world. After his death, China's leaders began a series of reforms.

Altay

• Yining

■ Urümqi

Tian Shan

Aksu

• Kashi

Taklimakan Desert

C

• Hotan

Kunlun Mts

Altun Mts

Tibetan Plateau

Himalayas

Lhasa
•

Everest
8848m

0		500 mile
0		500 kilometres

Guilin in southeastern China has some spectacular scenery. Natural crags of limestone rock rise above green rice fields. The rocks have sometimes been likened to dragons' teeth. In Chinese mythology, dragons are friendly not fearsome creatures.

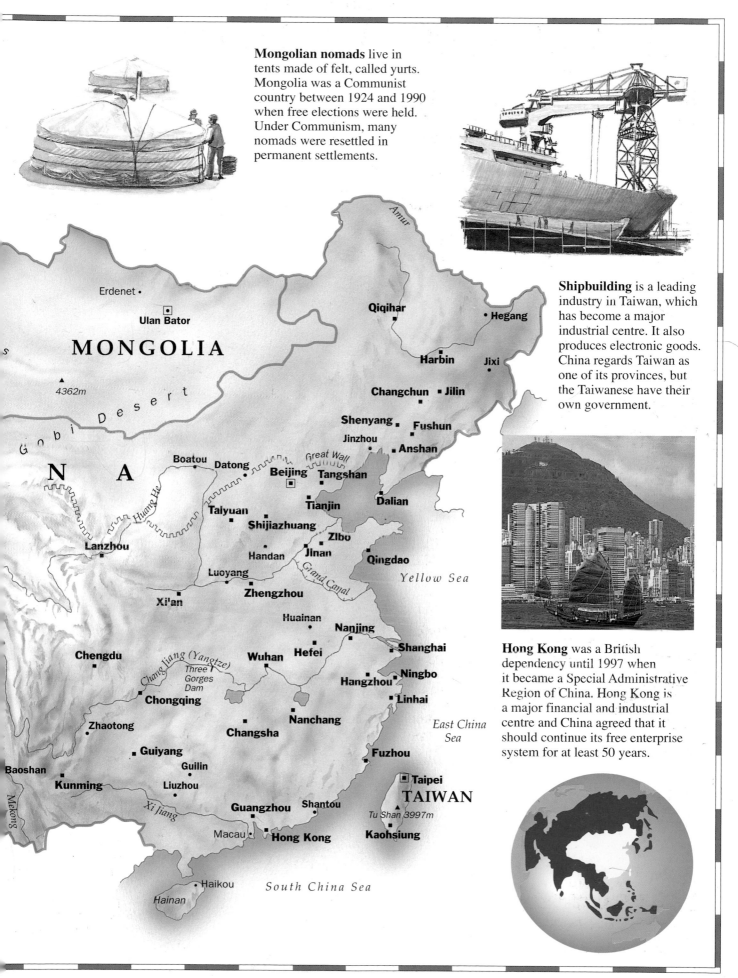

Mongolian nomads live in tents made of felt, called yurts. Mongolia was a Communist country between 1924 and 1990 when free elections were held. Under Communism, many nomads were resettled in permanent settlements.

Shipbuilding is a leading industry in Taiwan, which has become a major industrial centre. It also produces electronic goods. China regards Taiwan as one of its provinces, but the Taiwanese have their own government.

Hong Kong was a British dependency until 1997 when it became a Special Administrative Region of China. Hong Kong is a major financial and industrial centre and China agreed that it should continue its free enterprise system for at least 50 years.

Erdenet •

□ Ulan Bator

MONGOLIA

▲ 4362m

Gobi Desert

Qiqihar   • Hegang

Harbin   Jixi

Changchun • Jilin

Shenyang   Fushun
Jinzhou
    • Anshan

Boatou Datong   Great Wall
    Beijing Tangshan
N   A   Huang He
    Taiyuan   Tianjin   Dalian
        Shijiazhuang
    Lanzhou   Zibo
        Handan   Jinan
    Luoyang   Qingdao
            Grand Canal   *Yellow Sea*
    Xi'an   Zhengzhou

        Huainan
            Nanjing
Chengdu   Wuhan Hefei   • Shanghai
    Chang Jiang (Yangtze)
    Three   • Ningbo
    Gorges   Hangzhou
    Dam   Chongqing   • Linhai
Zhaotong   Nanchang   *East China*
        Changsha   *Sea*
    Guiyang
        Guilin   Fuzhou
Baoshan   Liuzhou
Kunming   □ Taipei
    Xi Jiang   **TAIWAN**
    Guangzhou Shantou   Tu Shan 3997m ▲
    Macau • **Hong Kong**   Kaohsiung

    • Haikou   *South China Sea*
    Hainan

Amur

Mekong

21

KOREAN PENINSULA

The Korean peninsula juts out from northeastern China, separating the Yellow Sea to the west from the Sea of Japan to the east. From 1910 the Korean peninsula was a Japanese colony. But in 1945, at the end of World War II, Russian troops occupied the northern part of the peninsula, while American forces occupied the south.

This division led to the creation of Communist North Korea and non-Communist South Korea. The two countries fought against each other between 1950 and 1953, when the present boundary was agreed. Tension between them continued throughout the second half of the 20th century. North Korea is less developed than South Korea, which is a fast-growing industrial country.

Kim Il Sung (1912-94) headed the government of North Korea, ruling as a dictator from 1948, when the Communist Democratic People's Republic was established, until his death in 1994. He was succeeded by his son, Kim Jong Il.

 SOUTH KOREA

Area: 99,274sq km (38,330sq miles)
Highest point: Halla 1,950m (6,398ft)
Population: 48,847,000
Capital and largest city: Seoul (pop 9,714,000)
Other large cities: Pusan (3,673,000)
Taegu (2,580,000)
Inchon (2,618,000)
Taejon (1,495,000)
Official language: Korean
Religions: Christianity (26%), Buddhism (26%)
Government: Republic
Currency: South Korean won

 NORTH KOREA

Area: 120,538sq km (46,540sq miles)
Highest point: Paektu 2,744m (9,003ft)
Population: 23,113,000
Capital and largest city: Pyongyang (pop 3,228,000)
Other large cities: Hamhung (565,000)
Nampo (455,000)
Chongjin (327,000)
Official language: Korean
Religions: Traditional beliefs, Chondogyo
Government: People's republic
Currency: North Korean won

Seoul, the capital of South Korea, is one of the world's largest cities. Modern skyscrapers show just how fast South Korea has developed since the 1950s. But the city still has many beautiful old buildings.

NORT

Sinuiju

Anju

Taedong

Pyongyang

Nampo

Haeju

Kaes

Inch

Yellow Sea

0   100 miles
0   100 kilometres

Cars and computers are among the many goods exported by South Korea. The country also ranks among the world's top ten producers of cement, commercial vehicles, steel, televisions and tyres.

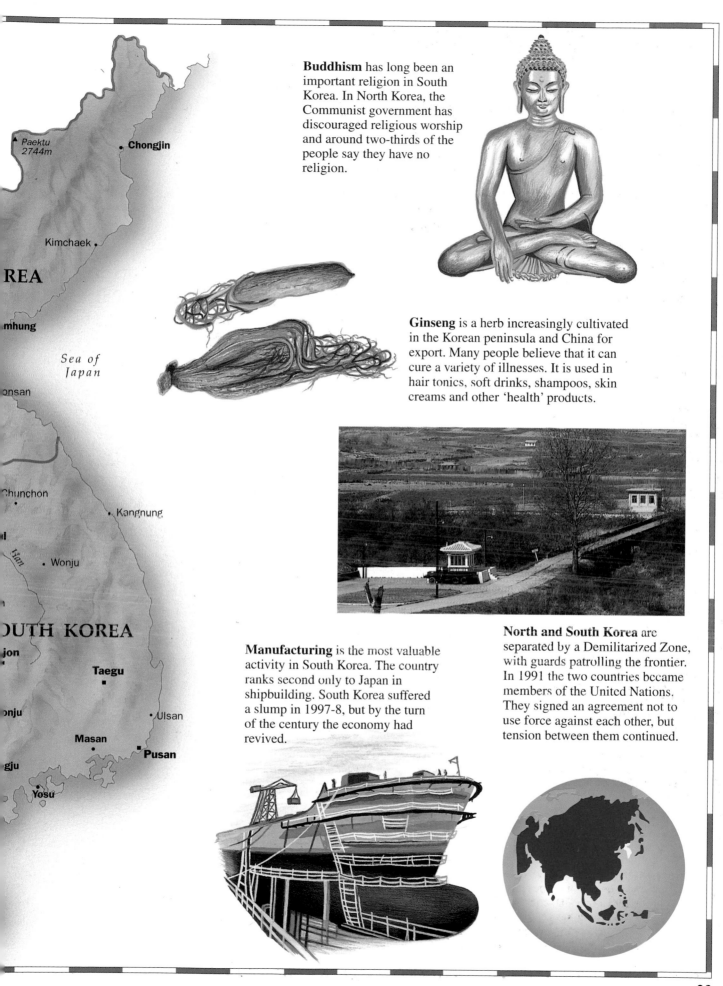

Buddhism has long been an important religion in South Korea. In North Korea, the Communist government has discouraged religious worship and around two-thirds of the people say they have no religion.

Ginseng is a herb increasingly cultivated in the Korean peninsula and China for export. Many people believe that it can cure a variety of illnesses. It is used in hair tonics, soft drinks, shampoos, skin creams and other 'health' products.

Manufacturing is the most valuable activity in South Korea. The country ranks second only to Japan in shipbuilding. South Korea suffered a slump in 1997-8, but by the turn of the century the economy had revived.

North and South Korea are separated by a Demilitarized Zone, with guards patrolling the frontier. In 1991 the two countries became members of the United Nations. They signed an agreement not to use force against each other, but tension between them continued.

Paektu 2744m

Chongjin

Kimchaek

REA

mhung

Sea of Japan

onsan

Chunchon

Kangnung

Wonju

Han

SOUTH KOREA

jon

Taegu

onju

Ulsan

Masan

Pusan

gju

Yosu

JAPAN

Japan consists of four large islands, which together make up 98 per cent of the country, and thousands of tiny islands. Much of the land is mountainous, but most people live on the small, fertile plains around the coast. Japan lies on an unstable part of the earth, called the Pacific 'ring of fire'. The country has more than 150 volcanoes, 60 of which are active, and earthquakes are common.

In 1945, after its defeat in World War II, Japan was in ruins. But it is now the world's second biggest economy after the United States. It imports most of the fuels and materials it needs for its huge industries, which have been successful largely through the hard work and skill of its workers and the use of modern technology.

 ## JAPAN

Area: 377,801sq km (145,870sq miles)
Highest point: Mount Fuji 3,776m (12,388ft)
Population: 127,464,000
Capital and largest city: Tokyo (pop 34,497,000)
Other large cities: Yokohama (3,604,000)
Osaka (2,590,000)
Nagoya (2,195,000)
Sapporo (1,896,000)
Kobe (1,535,000)
Kyoto (1,458,000)
Official language: Japanese
Religions: Shinto and related religions, including Buddhism (84%)
Government: Monarchy
Currency: Yen

Sumo is a Japanese form of wrestling in which the wrestler tries to throw his opponent to the ground or force him outside a 4.6-metre (15-ft) circle. Judo, karate and kendo (a form of fencing) are other popular sports in Japan.

Silkworms are the caterpillars, or larvae, of a moth. They feed on the leaves of the white mulberry tree. When fully grown, the silkworms spin a silken cocoon (outer wrapping) around themselves, which is the source of silk thread. Japan is one of the world's top silk producers.

Emperor Akihito is Japan's head of state. He succeeded his father Hirohito in 1989. Before World War II, the Japanese regarded Hirohito as a god. After the war, new laws made him a constitutional monarch.

Mount Fuji is a dormant (sleeping) volcano that last erupted in 1707-8. The snow-capped mountain is on the island of Honshu. The Japanese regard it as a sacred mountain.

Matsue .

Hiroshima

Oka

Kitakyushu

Inland Sea

Tok

Fukuoka

Matsuyama   Ko

Shikoku

Nagasaki

Kumamoto

Kyushu

Miyazaki

Kagoshima

PACIFIC OCEAN

Fish are an important part of the diet of Japanese people. Because farmland is scarce, Japan once lacked protein-rich foods, such as meat. Now, however, the people eat increasing amounts of meat and dairy products.

Wakkanai

Abashiri

Asahikawa

Hokkaido

Sapporo

Kushiro

Hakodate

North Pacific Ocean

Earthquakes cause great damage. In 1923 an earthquake hit the Tokyo-Yokohama area, killing about 143,000 people. In 1995 another earthquake struck the city of Kobe. More than 5,000 people died.

Aomori · Hachinohe

0 ⊢ 100 miles
0 ⊢ 100 kilometres

· Morioka

Akita

Sakata ·

Sea of Japan

Yamagata · **Sendai**

Niigata

Fukushima

Honshu

Calligraphy is the art of beautiful writing. The Japanese and Chinese regard it as an art. Written Japanese uses Chinese characters and Japanese phonetic symbols that represent sounds. Japanese is also written in the Roman alphabet.

Kanazawa

Hitachi

J A P A N

Motor cycles are produced in Japanese factories. Japan also leads the world in producing cars and ships, and is a major producer of commercial vehicles and electronic goods, such as computers, DVD and MP3 players, mobile telephones and home entertainment equipment.

Tokyo

Fuji 3776m ▲ **Kawasaki**

Kyoto **Nagoya** **Yokohama**

Osaka

Sakai **Hamamatsu**

ayama

Tokyo, the capital of Japan, is one of the world's largest cities. Its tall buildings and busy streets reflect its importance as Japan's chief business centre. But its parks, with their cherry trees, recall traditional Japan.

BANGLADESH, MYANMAR AND THAILAND

Bangladesh was once part of British India. In 1947 it became part of Pakistan and was called East Pakistan. In 1971 East Pakistan broke away and became the independent country of Bangladesh. Bangladesh is a poor but thickly populated country. It is often hit by floods which cause great human suffering.

Myanmar (formerly Burma) and Thailand are two of the countries in a region called Southeast Asia. Myanmar is another poor country which has been ruled by the military since 1962. Many people have criticized Myanmar's government for its bad human rights record. By contrast, in the second half of the 20th century, Thailand had become one of the wealthier countries in eastern Asia.

An earthquake in the Indian Ocean in 2004 caused a tsunami that devastated Thailand's coast and killed many people.

BANGLADESH

Area: 143,998sq km (55,598sq miles)
Highest point: Mt Keokradong 1,230m (4,034ft)
Population: 147,365,000
Capital and largest city: Dhaka (pop 11,560,000)
Other large cities: Chittagong (3,271,000)
Official language: Bengali
Religions: Islam (83%), Hinduism (16%)
Government: Republic
Currency: Taka

MYANMAR

Area: 676,578sq km (261,228sq miles)
Highest point: Hkakabo Razi 5,881m (19,296ft)
Population: 47,382,000
Capital and largest city: Yangon (pop 3,874,000)
Other large cities: Mandalay (1,237,000)
Official language: Burmese
Religions: Buddhism (89%), Christianity (5%), Islam (4%)
Government: Military regime
Currency: Kyat

THAILAND

Area: 513,115sq km (198,115sq miles)
Highest point: Inthanon Mountain 2,595m (8,514ft)
Population: 64,632,000
Capital and largest city: Bangkok (pop 6,486,000)
Official language: Thai
Religions: Buddhism (95%), Islam (4%)
Government: Monarchy
Currency: Baht

Floods are caused in Bangladesh when heavy rains make the rivers overflow. Other floods occur when tropical storms, called cyclones, hit the coast. Strong winds push seawater inland, flooding the flat coastal plains. Severe flooding was caused by a tsunami that swept the coast of Thailand in 2004.

Buddhist monks are a familiar sight in Myanmar and Thailand. In Myanmar most boys spend time in their local monastery. Some stay for a few weeks, others for years.

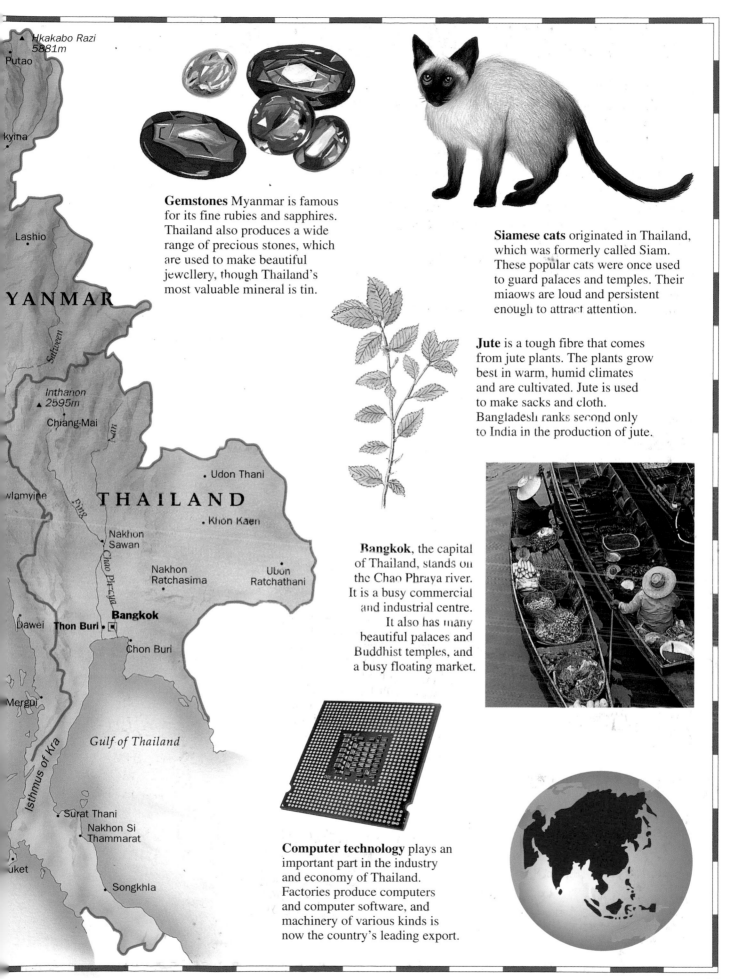

Gemstones Myanmar is famous for its fine rubies and sapphires. Thailand also produces a wide range of precious stones, which are used to make beautiful jewellery, though Thailand's most valuable mineral is tin.

Siamese cats originated in Thailand, which was formerly called Siam. These popular cats were once used to guard palaces and temples. Their miaows are loud and persistent enough to attract attention.

Jute is a tough fibre that comes from jute plants. The plants grow best in warm, humid climates and are cultivated. Jute is used to make sacks and cloth. Bangladesh ranks second only to India in the production of jute.

Bangkok, the capital of Thailand, stands on the Chao Phraya river. It is a busy commercial and industrial centre. It also has many beautiful palaces and Buddhist temples, and a busy floating market.

Computer technology plays an important part in the industry and economy of Thailand. Factories produce computers and computer software, and machinery of various kinds is now the country's leading export.

Hkakabo Razi
5881m
Putao
kyina
Lashio
YANMAR
Inthanon
2595m
Chiang-Mai
lamyine
THAILAND
Udon Thani
Khon Kaen
Nakhon Sawan
Nakhon Ratchasima
Ubon Ratchathani
Bangkok
Dawei Thon Buri
Chon Buri
Mergui
Gulf of Thailand
Isthmus of Kra
Surat Thani
Nakhon Si Thammarat
uket
Songkhla

CAMBODIA, LAOS AND VIETNAM

Cambodia, Laos and Vietnam form a region called Indochina. The region was ruled by France until 1954. Vietnam was divided into two parts: Communist North Vietnam and non-Communist South Vietnam. The division of Vietnam led to the Vietnam War (1957-75). Eventually, Vietnam was reunited as a single Communist country called the Socialist Republic of Vietnam.

Cambodia, Laos and Vietnam are poor developing countries that have been badly scarred by war. Most of their people depend on farming for their living. Manufacturing is increasing, especially in Vietnam.

CAMBODIA

Area: 181,035sq km (69,898sq miles)
Highest point: 1,813m (5,948ft) in west-central Cambodia
Population: 13,881,000
Capital and largest city: Phnom Penh (pop 1,157,000)
Official language: Khmer
Religions: Buddhism (95%)
Government: Republic
Currency: Riel

LAOS

Area: 236,800sq km (91,429sq miles)
Highest point: Mt Bia 2,817m (9,242ft)
Population: 6,368,000
Capital and largest city: Vientiane (pop 716,000)
Other large cities: Pakse (94,000) Savannakhet (68,000)
Official language: Lao
Religions: Buddhism (60%), local religions
Government: People's republic
Currency: Kip

VIETNAM

Area: 331,689sq km (128,066sq miles)
Highest point: Fan Si Pan 3,143m (10,312ft)
Population: 84,403,000
Capital: Hanoi (pop 3,977,000)
Largest cities: Ho Chi Minh City (3,497,000) Haiphong (612,000)
Official language: Vietnamese
Religions: Buddhism (10%), Christianity (9%)
Government: Socialist republic
Currency: Dong

Angkor Wat is a huge temple built in northern Cambodia in the 12th century in honour of the Hindu god Vishnu. It is perhaps the finest of the many ancient temples found in Cambodia.

Rice is the main food crop in all of the three countries in Indochina. The rice shoots are planted in the muddy soil in flooded fields. Rice grows well in the warm, humid climates of these countries.

Lao
Fan Si
314.

Luang Prabang

LAOS

Bia
2817m ▲

Mekong

Vientiane

0   100 miles
0   100 kilometres

Sisophon

Battambang

L.
Tonl

1813

Gulf of Thail...

Houses in Indochinese villages are often made of wood or bamboo and built on stilts. This keeps them dry when floods occur. About 80 per cent of the people of Indochina live in the countryside.

Durian is a fruit grown in Southeast Asia. The spherical fruit has a hard shell. The flesh has a pleasant sweet taste, but the fruit has a strong smell, like ripe cheese.

Mekong River
The Mekong, the longest river in Indochina, rises in Tibet. It forms part of the border between Thailand and Laos and then flows across Laos, Cambodia and Vietnam before emptying into the South China Sea near Ho Chi Minh City.

Ho Chi Minh (1890-1969) was a Vietnamese Communist, who led his country in the struggle for independence from France. He later served as president of Communist North Vietnam during the Vietnam War.

Giang

Lang Son •

Hanoi
□

oa Binh

• **Haiphong**

Ninh Binh

VIETNAM

• Vinh

South China Sea

Annamite Range

annakhet

Quang Tri •

• Hue

• **Da Nang**

Mekong

• Pakse

• Qui Nhon

• Stung Treng

AMBODIA

• Nha Trang

Kompong Cham

Da Lat •

• Cam Ranh

Penh • Tay Ninh

■ **Ho Chi Minh City**

Mekong

• My Tho

Gia

Can Tho

/lau

MALAYSIA, SINGAPORE AND BRUNEI

Malaysia is a large country. It includes the Malaysian peninsula, which is joined to mainland Asia, and two areas in northern Borneo called Sabah and Sarawak. This hot and rainy country has developed quickly since 1963, when Malaya, a British territory until 1957, agreed to unite with Singapore, Sabah and Sarawak.

Singapore, a small island country which was also once ruled by Britain, withdrew from Malaysia in 1965. It is now one of the most prosperous places in Asia. Brunei, a small country in Borneo, which became independent from Britain in 1984, is also prosperous. Its wealth comes from its rich oil reserves.

MALAYSIA

Area: 329,758sq km (127,320sq miles)
Highest point: Mt Kinabalu 4,094m (13,431ft)
Population: 24,386,000
Capital and largest city: Kuala Lumpur (pop 1,352,000)
Other large cities: Johor Baharu (839,000) Ipoh (692,000)
Official language: Malay
Religions: Islam (53%), Buddhism (17%)
Government: Federal monarchy
Currency: Ringgit

Singapore consists of one large island, also called Singapore, and 58 small ones. Its people are highly skilled and hardworking, and have made their country a major industrial centre. Trade and finance are also important.

SINGAPORE

Area: 618sq km (239sq miles)
Population: 4,492,000
Capital: Singapore (pop 4,253,000)
Official languages: Chinese, English, Malay, Tamil
Religions: Buddhism (43%), Islam (15%), Taoism (9%)
Government: Republic
Currency: Singaporean dollar

BRUNEI

Area: 5,765sq km (2,226sq miles)
Population: 379,000
Capital: Bandar Seri Begawan (pop 61,000)
Official language: Malay
Religions: Islam (67%), Buddhism (13%), Christianity (10%)
Government: Monarchy
Currency: Bruneian dollar

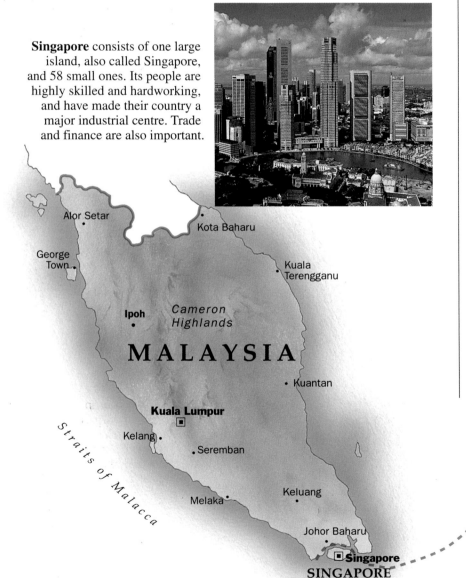

Alor Setar
Kota Baharu
George Town
Kuala Terengganu
Ipoh
Cameron Highlands
MALAYSIA
Kuantan
Kuala Lumpur
Kelang
Seremban
Straits of Malacca
Keluang
Melaka
Johor Baharu
Singapore
SINGAPORE

Exotic birds live in Malaysia, especially in the rainforests of Sabah and Sarawak. Malaysia has laws to protect wildlife and it has national parks where people can see the rich animal and plant life.

Palm oil and rubber Malaysia is the world's leading producer of palm oil which comes from the fruit of the oil palm. It also ranks among the world's major producers of natural rubber and cocoa, although cocoa was not grown commercially there until the 1950s.

Tin mining was the industry on which Malaysia's economic development was originally based. But in the last twenty years, production has declined and Malaysia ranks well behind the leading producers, China and Indonesia.

Oil Brunei's economy depends on oil production. Malaysia also produces oil. Oil, timber and tin are its leading natural resources. Rice is the chief crop, but manufacturing is now the most valuable activity in Malaysia.

Brunei is ruled by a Sultan who lives in a 1,700-room palace. Oil and natural gas were found in Brunei in 1929 and the nation became prosperous, making the Sultan the world's richest man. However, he lost at least half of his fortune in the 1980s and 1990s.

Kudat

Kota Kinabalu

Kinabalu 4094m

Sandakan

S a b a h

Bandar Seri Begawan

BRUNEI

Kuala Belait

Tawau

SOUTH CHINA SEA

Bintulu

MALAYSIA

Sibu

Rajang

S a r a w a k

Kuching

Bandar Sri Aman

0 — 100 miles

0 — 100 kilometres

31

INDONESIA AND EAST TIMOR

A mainly Muslim country, Indonesia is made up of about 13,600 islands, though fewer than 6,000 are inhabited. Most of the islands are mountainous and many mountains are active volcanoes. The bigger islands also have large coastal lowlands. The country has a hot and wet climate, with large rainforests.

Indonesia became independent from the Netherlands in 1949, but Portugal continued to rule the eastern part of the island of Timor until 1975. Indonesia ruled the area from 1976 until 1999, when the local people voted to make East Timor an independent country. It became independent in 2002.

Orang-utans are large apes that live in the forests of Borneo and Sumatra. They have recently been threatened by forest clearance and huge forest fires.

Banda Aceh

Medan

Pakanbaru

Sumatra

Padang

Mentawai Islands

Barisan Range

Bangka

Palembang

Belitung

INDIAN
OCEAN

Tanjungkarang

Pontianak

Sintang

*Kalimantan
(Borneo)*

Sama

Balikpapa

Banjarmasin

I N D

Java Sea

Krakatoa

Jakarta
Bekasi

Bogor

Semarang

Bandung *Java*

Surakarta

Surabaya

Yogyakarta

Malang

Bali

Lombo

Sum

INDONESIA

Area: 1,904,569sq km (735,358sq miles)
Highest point: Puncak Jaya 5,030m (16,503ft)
Population: 245,453,000
Capital and largest city: Jakarta
(pop 12,296,000)
Other large cities: Surabaya (2,367,000)
Medan (1,758,000)
Bandung (1,676,000)
Bekasi (1,569,000)
Palembang (1,250,000)
Official language: Bahasa Indonesia
Religions: Islam (88%), Christianity (8%)
Government: Republic
Currency: Indonesian rupiah

Tourism is an important activity in Indonesia. The island of Bali, with its beautiful beaches, its ancient Hindu culture and attractions such as classical dancing, is particularly popular. But tourism has been hit since 2002 by bombings in tourist areas.

Krakatoa was one of the many volcanic islands in Indonesia. In 1883 it exploded with great force. The explosion triggered a destructive wave called a tsunami which drowned 36,000 people on nearby Sumatra and Java. About two-thirds of the island disappeared.

Tsunami In December 2004, an undersea earthquake off the coast of Sumatra near Banda Aceh triggered a tsunami that struck the coast of Indonesia and other countries. It wiped out whole communities, killing more than 200,000 people in the region and making many more homeless.

Spices are an important crop in Indonesia. Rice is the chief food crop and coffee, palm oil, rubber, sugar cane, tea and tobacco are exported. Agriculture employs about 40 per cent of the work force.

EAST TIMOR

Area: 14,609sq km (5,641sq miles)
Highest point: Foto Tatamailau 2,963m (9,721ft)
Population: 1,063,000
Capital and largest city: Dili (49,000)
Official languages: Tetum, Portuguese
Religions: Roman Catholic (90%) Islam (4%)
Government: Republic
Currency: US dollar

Talaud Is

Celebes Sea

Sangihe Is

Manado

Halmahera

Waigeo

Manokwari

Sulawesi
(Celebes)

Ceram Sea

Ceram

New Guinea

Maoke Range

Jayapura

Kendari

Buru

Puncak Jaya
5030m

N E S I A

West
Papua

ung Pandang

Aru Is

Banda Sea

Flores Sea

Wetar

Flores

Dili ⊡ **EAST TIMOR**

Sumba

Foho Tatamailu
2963m

Timor

Kupang

0   100 miles

0   100 kilometres

33

PHILIPPINES

The Philippines consists of about 7,100 islands, about 1,000 of which are inhabited. The country lies in the Pacific 'ring of fire', so volcanic eruptions and earthquakes are common. Much of the land is mountainous. Agriculture employs about 35 per cent of the country's workers, and bananas, cocoa, coconuts, coffee, maize, rice (the staple food), sugar cane and tobacco are leading crops. Manufacturing is increasing.

Spain ruled the Philippines from 1565 until 1898, when the United States took over. Japan invaded the Philippines during World War II, but the country became fully independent in 1946.

 PHILIPPINES

Area: 300,000sq km (115,830sq miles)
Highest point: Mount Apo 2,954m (9,692ft)
Population: 89,469,000
Capital: Manila (pop 10,352,000)
Other large cities: Quezon City (2,174,000)
Davao (1,245,000)
Caloocan (1,178,000)
Cebu (719,000)
Official languages: Filipino, English
Religions: Christianity (Roman Catholic 81%, Protestant 10%), Islam 5%
Government: Republic
Currency: Philippine peso

Christianity Spain claimed the Philippines in 1565 and missionaries soon began to convert the people to Christianity. As a result, the Philippines has more Christians than any other Asian country. Here Roman Catholics gather for an open-air Communion rally.

Forests cover about one-third of the land in the Philippines. Some hardwood trees known as Philippine mahoganies provide valuable timber. The country also produces bamboo and kapok, a fibre used in upholstery.

Laoag
Apa
South China Sea
Luzon
Cagayan
Dagupan
PHILIPPINES
• Tarlac
• Angeles
Caloocan
Olongapo
Quezon
Manila
San F
Batangas
Mindoro
• Puerto Princesa
Palawan
Sulu Sea
Balabac

0	100 miles
0	100 kilometres

Zambo
Bas
Jolo
Tawi-Tawi

Ferdinand Marcos (1917-89) was president of the Philippines from 1965 until 1986. Accused of corruption and election fraud, he fled the country in 1986. The Philippines faces several political problems including conflict with Muslim guerrillas, crime and unemployment.

ACIFIC OCEAN

Catanduanes

Naga

▲ Mayon Volcano
2421m

Masbate

Samar

ay

Tacloban

Cebu   Leyte

Bacolod

• Cebu

Dinagat

Bohol

Siargao

ros

• Butuan

Dipolog   • Cagayan de Oro

Mindanao

Pagadian

Datu Piang   Davao ■

Apo
2954m

General Santos

Jeepneys are a popular means of transport in the Philippines. These highly decorated shared taxis provide cheap transport for their passengers, who are crammed in. Buses are also important.

Manila, the capital of the Philippines, is also the country's chief commercial and cultural centre, as well as being the main port. It is a beautiful city on the shores of Manila Bay on Luzon island, but it has many slums where people live in desperate poverty.

Philippine eagles are also called monkey-eating eagles. They are found only in the Philippines. These eagles eat not just monkeys but also other mammals, birds and reptiles. They are becoming scarce because the rainforest trees in which they nest are being cut down.

Sugar cane grows well in the fertile, volcanic soils of the Philippines. Sugar cane is a plant that belongs to the grass family. Its stalks contain a sweet juice from which sugar and syrup are made.

PEOPLE AND BELIEFS

More than 60 per cent of the world's people live in Asia. Vast areas are too dry, too cold or too mountainous for people to live in them. By contrast, some parts of eastern, southeastern and southern Asia are among the most densely populated places in the world. Many people live in huge cities. Asia's largest cities include Tokyo (Japan), Jakarta (Indonesia), Seoul (South Korea), Mumbai, (India), Shanghai (China) and Delhi (India).

The Dome of the Rock mosque rises above the Wailing Wall in Jerusalem. Islam, Hinduism and Buddhism are the main faiths in Asia. There are fewer than five million Jews.

Population densities in Asia

Number of people
per square kilometre

■	Over 100
■	Between 50 and 100
■	Between 10 and 50
■	Between 1 and 10
■	Below 1

■ Cities of more than 1,000,000 people

• Cities of more than 500,000 people

Population and area

Although only 75 per cent of Russia lies in Asia, it is Asia's largest country. The next largest countries in Asia are China, India, Kazakhstan (a small proportion of which is in Europe), Saudi Arabia and the island country of Indonesia.

China and India have more people than any other countries in the world. Indonesia ranks fourth, after the United States. Russia ranks sixth in population, but about 80 per cent of Russia's population lives in European Russia. Pakistan, Bangladesh and Japan also have huge populations.

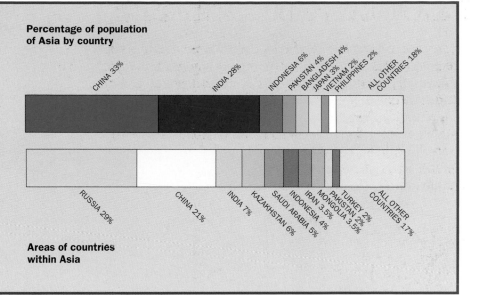

Percentage of population of Asia by country

CHINA 33% · INDIA 28% · INDONESIA 6% · PAKISTAN 4% · BANGLADESH 4% · JAPAN 3% · VIETNAM 2% · PHILIPPINES 2% · ALL OTHER COUNTRIES 18%

RUSSIA 29% · CHINA 21% · INDIA 7% · KAZAKHSTAN 6% · SAUDI ARABIA 5% · INDONESIA 4% · IRAN 3.5% · MONGOLIA 3.5% · PAKISTAN 2% · TURKEY 2% · ALL OTHER COUNTRIES 17%

Areas of countries within Asia

Main religions

All the world's major religions were founded in Asia. Judaism, Christianity and Islam all began in southwestern Asia. Today, most people in southwestern Asia are Muslims, but Judaism is the chief religion in Israel and Christianity the chief religion in Cyprus. Hinduism began in India and, today, more than four-fifths of the people of India are Hindus. But Muslims make up about 13 per cent of the people of India, while Islam is also the chief religion in Bangladesh, the Maldives and Pakistan. Buddhism, which began in India about 2,500 years ago, has spread into much of eastern Asia. Islam is the chief religion of Brunei, Indonesia and Malaysia, while Christianity is the main religion in the Philippines. Some local religions survive in remote areas in Indonesia. Confucianism is important in eastern Asia, while Shinto is followed in Japan.

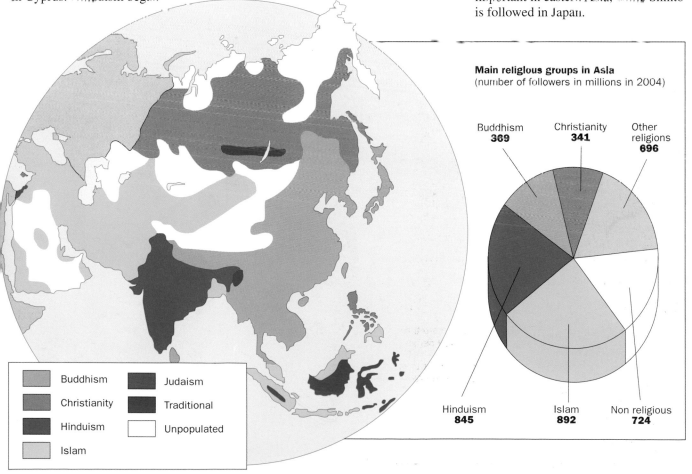

Buddhism
Christianity
Hinduism
Islam
Judaism
Traditional
Unpopulated

Main religious groups in Asia
(number of followers in millions in 2004)

Buddhism **369**
Christianity **341**
Other religions **696**
Hinduism **845**
Islam **892**
Non religious **724**

CLIMATE AND VEGETATION

Asia's climates range from polar and tundra in the north, to hot tropical in the south. South of the polar region, much of Siberia, in northern Asia, has a cold climate, with vast coniferous forests of fir, pine and spruce. In eastern Asia, these forests merge into mixed forest, with tropical forests in the southeast and parts of India. Central Asia has grassy steppe and cold deserts, while hot deserts cover much of southwestern Asia.

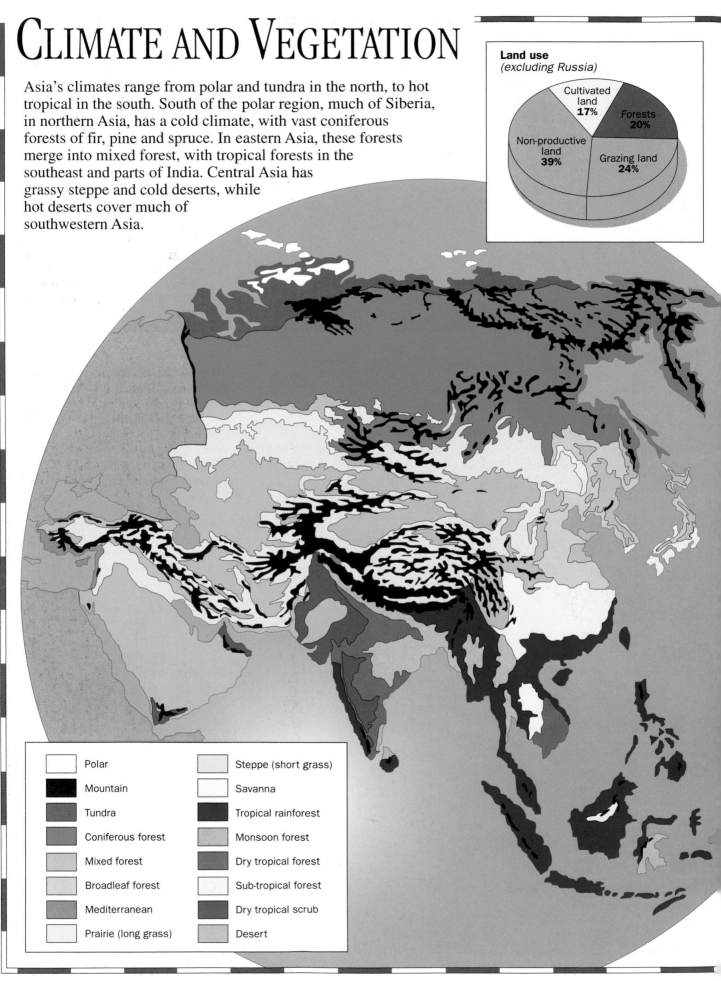

Land use
(excluding Russia)

- Cultivated land **17%**
- Forests **20%**
- Grazing land **24%**
- Non-productive land **39%**

Legend:
- Polar
- Mountain
- Tundra
- Coniferous forest
- Mixed forest
- Broadleaf forest
- Mediterranean
- Prairie (long grass)
- Steppe (short grass)
- Savanna
- Tropical rainforest
- Monsoon forest
- Dry tropical forest
- Sub-tropical forest
- Dry tropical scrub
- Desert

Winter temperatures

Summer temperatures

Temperature
key scale in °C

- below–32
- –32 to –24
- –24 to –16
- –16 to –8
- –8 to 0
- 0 to 8
- 8 to 16
- 16 to 24
- 24 to 32
- Above 32

Range of climates

Temperature and precipitation (rain, snow and all other forms of moisture that come from the air) are the two main factors that determine climate. Asia's climate varies from the Arctic north to the equatorial regions in the southeast. The climate is influenced by the distance a place is from the sea. Extreme climates, with hot summers and bitterly cold winters and little precipitation, occur in central Asia.

In southern Asia, winds blow outwards from the land to the sea in winter. In summer, the land heats up and moist air is drawn inland from the sea. This causes a reversal of wind directions. These seasonal winds are called monsoons.

Rainfall

Monsoons bring heavy rain to India and other areas in summer. Indonesia has rain throughout the year, while southwestern Asia has a hot desert climate. Life is possible only at oases – places where water is available.

Floods and droughts

Heavy monsoon rains sometimes make rivers overflow, causing floods. When the monsoon winds are late or fail to bring enough rain, droughts may occur. Crops fail and people may suffer starvation.

Annual rainfall
In mm

- Above 3000
- 2000 - 3000
- 1000 - 2000
- 500 - 1000
- 250 - 500
- 0 - 250

ECOLOGY AND ENVIRONMENT

Currently Asia's population is increasing every year by more than 50 million. Many parts of Asia are overcrowded and, as the population increases, overcrowding grows worse. The yearly increase in population creates pressure on the land, with rainforests being cleared to provide timber and fuel, and land for farming and human settlement. In some areas, the cutting down of trees has led to environmental disasters and a great reduction in the numbers of wild animals and plants. Unknown numbers of plant species, some that might have been of medicinal value, become extinct all the time.

Rice is harvested on land that was once rainforest. The people need the food, but the environmental cost is unknown.

Environmental damage to land and sea

- Existing desert
- Area at risk of desertification
- Present rainforest
- Rainforest seriously damaged in recent years
- Most polluted seas
- Most polluted rivers
- Area most affected by acid rain
- Serious pollution from cities

Damaging the environment

When forests in upland areas are cut down, the effects are felt in the lowlands. Without trees to soak up the water and anchor the soil, the rain flows over the surface, washing away fertile soils. The soil is swept into the swollen rivers, where it piles up on the river beds. This makes the rivers overflow their banks, causing floods. Serious floods occurred in India in 2005.

In the late 1990s, forest fires in Indonesia, many deliberately started to clear the land, caused clouds of smoke that choked people in countries to the north, such as Malaysia and Singapore.

In Asia's overcrowded cities, factories and cars fill the air with gases, causing severe air pollution. Factories also tip harmful chemicals into rivers, making the water poisonous. Human populations use the river water for washing and also for disposing of waste. But the rivers are unable to cope with the amount of pollution and clean water is becoming increasingly scarce.

Natural hazards

Earthquakes occur in a band stretching from Turkey to the Himalayas. Earthquakes and volcanic eruptions are also common in southeastern and eastern Asia, which forms part of the Pacific 'ring of fire' where movements between the earth's crustal plates occur. In 2004 an undersea earthquake off the coast of Sumatra created a huge wave, called a tsunami, which flooded coastal areas of 12 Indian Ocean nations and killed more than 200,000 people.

Tropical storms, which drive seawater inland, causing floods, are another hazard facing the poor in southern and southeastern Asia. In 1970, a storm in Bangladesh killed about a million people.

Endangered species

The natural habitats of many animals have been greatly reduced as the human population has increased. Many kinds of animals are now endangered. The most famous example is the giant panda, the symbol of the WWF (formerly World Wide Fund for Nature). It lives in what remains of the cold forests in China's Sichuan province. Most of the trees and bamboos have been cut down by local people to build homes and for firewood.

Many animals, such as tigers and monkeys, are hunted by poachers for their skins and for body parts that are used in folk medicines. Some, including orang-utans, are caught as babies and sold as pets. Orang-utans have also been threatened by forest clearance and uncontrolled fires. Some species, including the large birdwing butterflies and many rainforest trees, are now protected.

Javan rhinoceros

Some endangered species of Asia

Mammals and reptiles
Asian elephant
Giant panda
Javan and Sumatran rhinos
Orang-utan
Snow leopard
Tiger
Komodo dragon
Marine turtles

Birds
Gurney's pitta
Japanese crane
Philippine monkey-eating eagle
Rothschild's mynah

Plants and trees
Blue vanda orchid
Dove tree
Paphiopedilum orchid
Rafflesia arnoldii

Earthquake zone
▲ Active volcanoes
Recent major earthquakes
Recent flood disasters
Major tropical storms

ECONOMY

More than half the people of Asia make their living by farming. Many farmers are poor and grow little more than they need to feed their families. The use of machinery, fertilizers and new, higher-producing seeds of such crops as rice and wheat, have raised production in recent years. Japan is a major industrial power and manufacturing is increasing, especially in eastern Asia, from Indonesia to Korea.

All over Asia old-fashioned factories are being modernized to cope with increasing trade with the rest of the world.

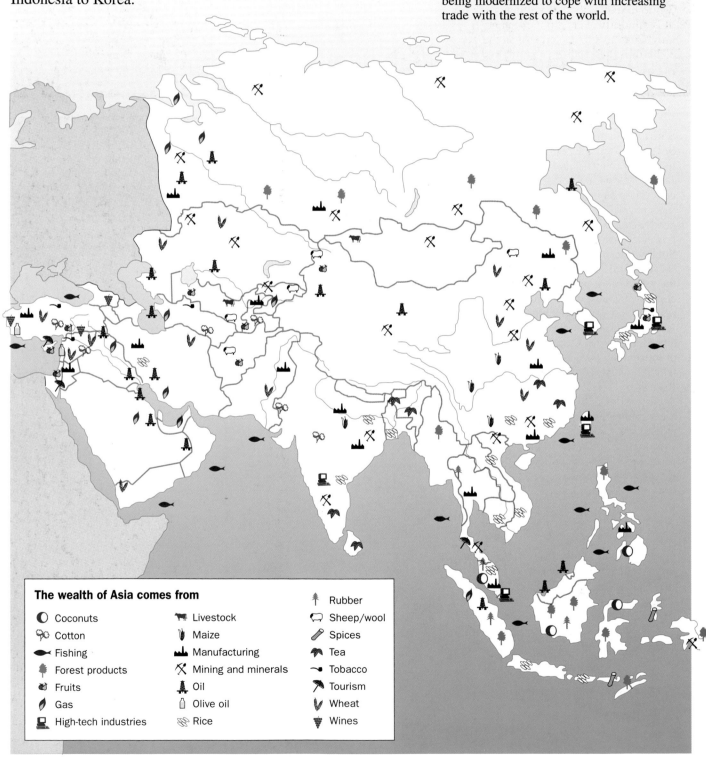

The wealth of Asia comes from

- ☾ Coconuts
- 🐏 Cotton
- 🐟 Fishing
- 🌲 Forest products
- 🍓 Fruits
- 🍃 Gas
- 💻 High-tech industries
- 🐄 Livestock
- 🌾 Maize
- 🏭 Manufacturing
- ⚒ Mining and minerals
- 🛢 Oil
- 🍶 Olive oil
- 🌾 Rice
- 🌴 Rubber
- 🐑 Sheep/wool
- 🌶 Spices
- 🍃 Tea
- 🚬 Tobacco
- ⛏ Tourism
- 🌽 Wheat
- 🍇 Wines

Gross domestic product

In order to compare the economies of countries, experts work out the gross domestic product (GDP) of the country in US dollars. The GDP is the total value of the goods and services produced by a country in a year. The chart shows that Japan has the highest GDP. Its GDP ranks second only in the world to that of the United States. It is almost twice that of China and more than five times larger than the GDP of India.

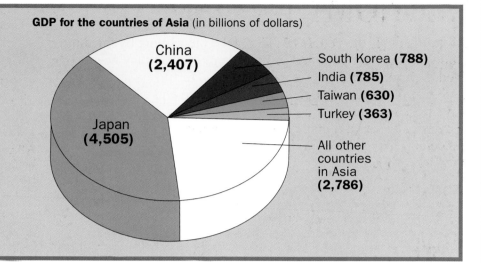

GDP for the countries of Asia (in billions of dollars)

China (2,407)
South Korea (788)
India (785)
Taiwan (630)
Turkey (363)
All other countries in Asia (2,786)
Japan (4,505)

Sources of energy

Several of Asia's leading industrial countries, including Japan, lack oil, natural gas and coal. They have to import these fuels to produce the energy they need. Several Asian countries are, however, major fuel producers. Southwestern Asia is a leading source of oil. Saudi Arabia leads the world in oil production and it contains the largest known reserves. Iran and the United Arab Emirates also ranked among the world's top ten producers in 2005, as did Russia, which now rivals Saudi Arabia. Russia, Iran, Indonesia, Saudi Arabia and Uzbekistan are also major producers of natural gas. China leads the world in coal production, while India, Russia and Kazakhstan are other leading coal producers.

Per capita GDPs

Per capita means per head or per person. Per capita GDPs are worked out by dividing the GDP by the population. Japan has the highest per capita GDP in Asia, but tiny Singapore, with its many industries, also has a high per capita GDP. Countries with low per capita GDPs are Afghanistan, Cambodia, Nepal and Yemen.

Sources of energy found in Asia

🛢 Oil
💧 Gas
≈ Hydroelectricity
⚒ Coal
☢ Uranium

POLITICS AND HISTORY

The world map is always changing. From the 1940s, country after country in Asia became independent. In 1947 British India was divided into India and Pakistan. These two countries still dispute their boundaries. In 1991 the nations of Kazakhstan, Kyrgyzstan, Tajikistan, Turkmenistan and Uzbekistan were created when the Soviet Union split up. In 1997, British Hong Kong became part of China and, in 2002, East Timor broke away from Indonesia to become an independent nation.

Great events

The oldest known civilizations were founded in Mesopotamia in what is now Iraq. Other great civilizations grew up in the Indus River valley and in China. Asia was also the birthplace of the world's major religions.

Contact with Europe increased rapidly from the early 16th century when the Portuguese found new sea routes from Europe to Asia. Then came Spanish, Dutch and British traders and missionaries. By the 19th century, European powers had colonized much of Asia. In the late 19th and early 20th centuries, Japan emerged as a military power, but it was finally defeated in 1945 when the first atomic bombs were dropped on the country.

In the late 1940s, several Asian countries became independent and, in 1949, a Communist government took over in China. The spread of Communism led to wars in Korea (1950-3) and Vietnam (1954-75). Japan, with help from the United States, recovered to become a major world economic power. From the 1970s, several countries, including Hong Kong (part of China since 1997), South Korea, Singapore, Taiwan and Thailand, and more recently China itself, have built up their economies, but many Asians remain poor.

The 21st century has seen a rise in terrorism resulting in wars in Afghanistan and Iraq. The restoration of peace and the fight against poverty are Asia's main challenge.

Great Asian empires

- Assyrian 700 BC
- Ch'in 200 BC
- Mongol 1300
- Mughal 1700

Important dates

8350 Jericho founded – the world's first walled city

6000 First known pottery and textiles at Çatal Hüyük (Turkey)

3500 Mesopotamian empires founded in Iraq

3100 First writing on clay tablets from Mesopotamia

2750 Growth of Indus Valley civilizations

2500 Horses domesticated in central Asia

1700s Huang He and Yangtze civilizations in China

1600 Rise of Shang dynasty in China

720 Height of Assyrian Empire

660 Jimmu, first emperor of Japan

486 Death of Siddhartha Gautama, founder of Buddhism

300s Empire of Alexander the Great

214 Great Wall of China begun

200s Ch'in Empire in China

AD 30 Jesus of Nazareth, founder of Christianity, crucified in Jerusalem

100s Han Empire of China

300s Gupta Empire of China

407 Start of first Mongol Empire

625 Islam founded by the Prophet Mohammed

700s Tang Empire of China

730 First printing in China

939 Civil wars in Japan

1096 First crusades to the Holy Land

1206 Genghis Khan conquered largest empire in history

1275 Marco Polo established merchant route by land from Europe to China

1368 Ming dynasty founded in China

1516 Height of Ottoman (Turkish

1526 Foundation of Empire in Ind

8000 BC · AD 1 · 1500

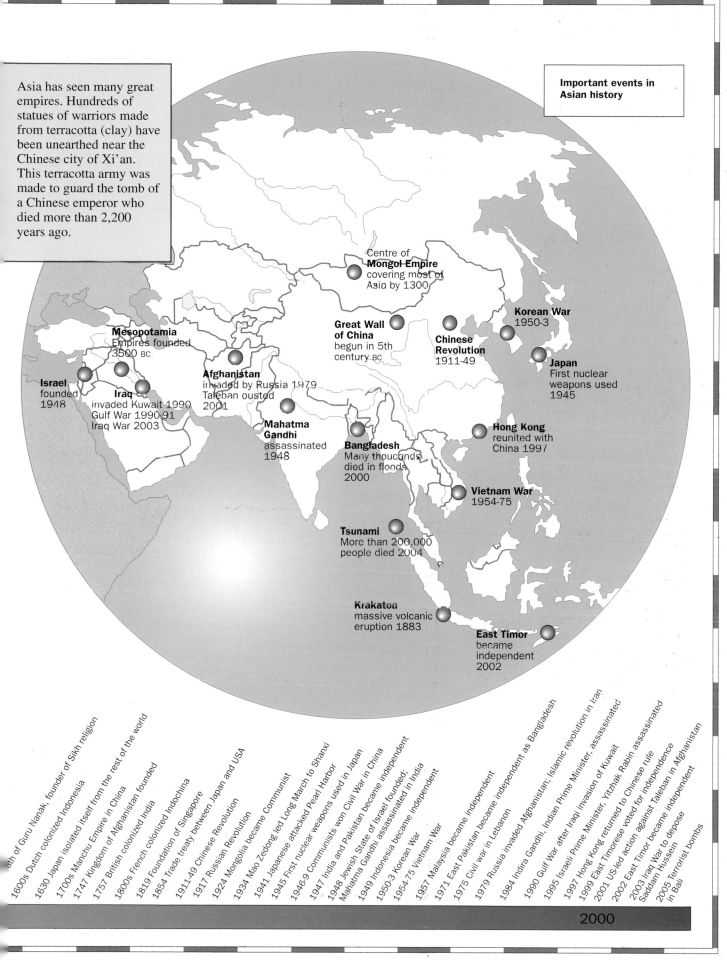

Important events in Asian history

Asia has seen many great empires. Hundreds of statues of warriors made from terracotta (clay) have been unearthed near the Chinese city of Xi'an. This terracotta army was made to guard the tomb of a Chinese emperor who died more than 2,200 years ago.

Centre of **Mongol Empire** covering most of Asia by 1300

Great Wall of China begun in 5th century BC

Chinese Revolution 1911-49

Korean War 1950-3

Japan First nuclear weapons used 1945

Mesopotamia Empires founded 3500 BC

Israel founded 1948

Iraq invaded Kuwait 1990 Gulf War 1990-91 Iraq War 2003

Afghanistan invaded by Russia 1979 Taleban ousted 2001

Mahatma Gandhi assassinated 1948

Bangladesh Many thousands died in floods 2000

Hong Kong reunited with China 1997

Vietnam War 1954-75

Tsunami More than 200,000 people died 2004

Krakatoa massive volcanic eruption 1883

East Timor became independent 2002

th of Guru Nanak, founder of Sikh religion
1600s Dutch colonized Indonesia
1630 Japan isolated itself from the rest of the world
1700s Manchu Empire in China
1747 Kingdom of Afghanistan founded
1757 British colonized India
1800s French colonized Indochina
1819 Foundation of Singapore
1854 Trade treaty between Japan and USA
1911-49 Chinese Revolution
1917 Russian Revolution
1924 Mongolia became Communist
1934 Mao Zedong led Long March to Shanxi
1941 Japanese attacked Pearl Harbor
1945 First nuclear weapons used in Japan
1946-9 Communists won Civil War in China
1947 India and Pakistan became independent
1948 Jewish State of Israel founded; Mahatma Gandhi assassinated in India
1949 Indonesia became independent
1950-3 Korean War
1954-75 Vietnam War
1957 Malaysia became independent
1971 East Pakistan became independent as Bangladesh
1975 Civil war in Lebanon
1979 Russia invaded Afghanistan; Islamic revolution in Iran
1984 Indira Gandhi, Indian Prime Minister, assassinated
1990 Gulf War after Iraqi invasion of Kuwait
1995 Israeli Prime Minister, Yitzhak Rabin assassinated
1997 Hong Kong returned to Chinese rule
1999 East Timorese voted for independence
2001 US-led action against Taleban in Afghanistan
2002 East Timor became independent
2003 Iraq War to depose Saddam Hussein
2005 Terrorist bombs in Bali

2000

INDEX

Numbers in **bold** are map references
Numbers in *italics* are picture references

A
Abadan **12**
Abashiri **25**
Abha **11**
Abu Dhabi **11**
Adana **9**
Adapazari **8**
Aden **11**
Aegean Sea **8**
Afghanistan **4**, 16, **16–17**
statistics 16
Afyon **8**
Agra **18**, *19*
agriculture *see* farming
Ahmadabad **18**
Ahvas **12**
Ajmer **18**
Akihito, Emperor *24*
Akita **25**
Aksu **20**
Al Amarah **12**
Aleppo **9**
Alexander the Great *12*
Al Hillah **12**
Al Hudaydah **11**
Al Hufuf **11**
Aligarh **18**
Al Jawf **10**
Al Khaburah **11**
Allahabad **19**
Al Masira **11**
Almaty **15**
Al Mukalla **11**
Alor Setar **30**
Altai Mountains **7**, **20–1**
Altun Mountains **20**
Altay **20**
Al Wajh **10**
Amman **9**
Amritsar **18**
Amudarya River **14–15**, **16–17**
Amur River **7**, **21**
Anadyr River **7**
Andijon **15**
Angarsk **7**
Angeles **34**
Angkor **28**
Angkor Wat *28*
animals *5*
    Arabian peninsula *10*, *11*
    China *20*
    endangered species *5*, *10*, *20*, 41, *41*
    Indonesia *32*
    Russia and the Caucasus *6*
    sacred *19*
    see also individual species
Anju **22**
Ankara **9**
An Nafud **10**
An Najaf **12**
Annamite Range **29**
Anshan **21**
Antakya **9**
Antalya **8**
Aomori **25**
Aparri **34**
Apo (mountain) **35**
Aqaba **9**
Aqtau **14**
Aqtöbe **14**
Arabian Gulf *see* Gulf, The
Arabian peninsula 10–11, **10–11**
Arabian Sea **11**, **16–17**, 18
Aragats (mountain) **6**
Arak **13**
Aral **15**
Aral Sea *14*, **14–15**, *15*
Ararat (mountain) **9**

Aras River **12**
Arctic Ocean **7**
Ardabil **12**
Armenia **4**, 6, *6*
    statistics 6
Ar Ramadi **12**
Aru Islands **33**
Asahikawa **25**
Asanol **19**
Ashgabat **14**
Asia 4–5, **4–5**
    largest cities 36
    largest countries 37
    statistics 5
Assad Reservoir **9**
Assyria *12*, *44*
Astana *14*, **15**
At Taif **10**
Atyrau **14**
Aurangabad **18**
Aydin **8**
Azerbaijan **4**, 5, 6, *6*
    statistics 6

B
Babylon *12*
Bacolod **35**
Baghdad **12**
Baghlan **17**
Bago **26**
Bahawalpur **17**
Bahrain **4**, 10, **11**
    statistics 10
Bakhtaran **12**
Baku **6**
Balabac (island) **34**
Bali (island) **32**, *32*
Balikpapan **32**
Balkhash, Lake **15**
Baluchistan Plateau **16**
Bam **13**
bamboo *34*
bananas *34*
Banda Aceh **32**
Banda Sea **33**
Bandar Abbas **13**
Bandar Seri Begawan **31**
Bandar Sri Aman **31**
Bandung **32**
Bangalore **18**
Bangka (island) **32**
Bangkok *27*, **27**
Bangladesh **4–5**, 26, **26**
    statistics 26
Banjarmasin **32**
Bannu **17**
Baoshan **21**
Bareilly **18**
Barisan Range **32**
Barnaul **7**
Basilan (island) **34**
Basra **12**
Batangas **34**
Battambang **28**
bauxite *6*
Baykal, Lake **7**
Baykonur **15**, *15*
Bazar Dyuzi (mountain) **6**
Beersheba **9**
Beijing **21**
Beirut **9**
Belitung (island) **32**
Bengal, Bay of **19**, **26**
Bergama **8**
Bering Sea **7**
Beysehir, Lake **8**
Bhagalpur **19**
Bhavnagar **18**
Bhopal **18**
Bhutan **4**, 18, **19**

statistics 18
Bia (mountain) **28**
Bikaner **18**
Bilaspur **19**
Bintulu **31**
birds:
    endangered 41
    Malaysian *31*
    Philippines *35*
Bishkek **15**
Black Sea **4**, **6**, 8, **8–9**
Boatou **21**
Bogor **32**
Bohol (island) **35**
Bombay *see* Mumbai
borders:
    Asia-Europe 4
    disputed *17*, 44
    Kashmir 17
    North/South Korea *23*
    Thailand and Laos *29*
Borneo (island) **32–3**
Bosporus **8**
Brahmaputra River **19**, **26**
Bratsk **7**
Brunei **5**, 30, **31**
    royal palace *31*
    statistics 30
Buddhism *4*, *23*, 36, 37, **37**
    monks *26*
    temples *27*
Bukhara **15**
Buraydah **11**
Burma *see* Myanmar
Bursa **8**
Buru (island) **33**
Bushehr **13**
Butuan **35**

C
Ca Mau **29**
Cagayan de Oro **35**
Cagayan River **34**
Calcutta *see* Kolkata
calligraphy *25*
Caloocan **34**
Cam Ranh **29**
Cambodia **5**, 28, **28–9**
    statistics 28
camels:
    Arabian *11*
    Bactrian *17*
Cameron Highlands **30**
Can Tho **7**
car production *25*
carpets, Persian *13*
Caspian Sea **4**, 6, **6**, **12–13**, *14*
Catanduanes (island) **35**
cattle *15*, *19*
Caucasus *see* Russia and the Caucasus
Caucasus Mountains *4*, 6
Cebu (city) **35**
Cebu (island) **35**
Cedar of Lebanon *9*
Celebes Sea **33**
Central Asia 14–15, **14–15**
Central Siberian Plateau **7**
Ceram (island) **33**
Ceram Sea **33**
Ceylon *18*
chador *10*
Chah Bahar **13**
Chandigarh **18**
Changchun **21**
Changsha **21**
Chao Phraya River **27**
Chariker **17**
Chechnya *6*
Cheju (island) **22-3**
Chelyabinsk **6**
Chenab River *17*, **17**
Chengdu **21**
Chennai **18**
Chiang-Mai **27**

China **4–5**, 20–1, **20–1**
    Great Wall *5*, **21**
    mythology *20*
    religions *4*
    Shanxi earthquake *41*
    statistics 20
Chita **7**
Chittagong **26**
Chonan **23**
Chon Buri **27**
Chongjin **23**
Chongqing **21**
Chonju **23**
Christianity *4*, 34, 37, **37**
    Philippines *34*
Chunchon **23**
climate 38–9, **39**
    Indonesia 32
coal production *43*, **43**
cocoa 31
coconuts *34*, **42**
coffee *33*, *34*
Coimbatore **18**
Colombo **19**
communism *see* politics
computer technology *22*, *27*
Confucianism *4*
copper *6*
Corum **9**
cotton *14*, *15*, **42**
craft industries *13*
cuneiform *4*
Cuttack **19**
cyclones 26
Cyprus **4**, 8, **8–9**
    statistics 8

D
Da Lat **29**
Da Nang **29**
Da River **28–9**
Dagupan **34**
Dalian **21**
Damascus **9**
Damavand (mountain) **13**
Damman **11**
Dardanelles **8**
Darjiling **19**
Dasht-e Kavir **13**
Dasht-e Lut **13**
dates *11*
Datong **21**
Datu Piang **35**
Davao **35**
Dawei **27**
Dayr az Zawr **9**
Dead Sea **9**
Deccan Plateau *18*, **18**
Dehra Dun **18**
Delhi *18*, 36
Denizil **8**
deserts: *4*
    Arabian peninsula *10*, **11**, *11*
    Central Asia 14, **14–15**, *15*
    China and Mongolia **20–1**
    India *18*
    Iraq *12*
    Mediterranean Asia *8*, **9**
    Syrian **9**, *12*
Dezful **12**
Dhaka **26**
Dhufar **11**
diamonds *6*
Dinagat (island) **35**
Dickson **7**
Dili **33**
Dipolog **35**
Diyarbakir **9**
Doha **11**
Dome of the Rock *36*
droughts 16, 39
Dubai **11**
durian fruit *29*
Dushanbe **15**

E
eagles, Philippine *35*, 41
earthquakes 7, *8*, *17*, 24, *25*, 26, 34, 41, **41**
East China Sea **21**
East Pakistan 26
East Siberian Sea **7**
East Timor **5**, **32**, 33, **33**, 45
Eastern Ghats (mountains) **18-19**
ecology **40**, 40–1
economy 5, 16, 42, **42**
    Arabian peninsula 11
    Bangladesh, Myanmar and Thailand 27
    Central Asia 14
    China 20
    Indonesia 32
    Japan 24, 25
    Korean peninsula 22, 23
    Malaysia and Brunei 31
    Mediterranean Asia 9
    Philippines 34
    Russia and the Caucasus 6
    Taiwan 21
Edremit **8**
Egridir, Lake **8**
Elat **9**
Elazig **9**
Elbrus (mountain) **6**
Elburz Mountains **13**
electronic goods 21, 25
'Empty Quarter' *see* Rub al Khali
energy sources 43, **43**
environmental problems 14, 40-1
Erdenet **21**
Erzincan **9**
Erzurum **9**
Esfahan **13**
Eskisehir **8**
Euphrates River **9**, *12*, **12**
Europe 4
Everest (mountain) **19**, *19*, 20

F
Faisalabad **17**
Faizabad **19**
Fan Si Pan (mountain) **28**
farming: 42
    Afghanistan and Pakistan *16*
    Arabian peninsula 10
    Central Asia 15
    Indochina 28
    Indonesia 33
    irrigation *17*
    Israel *9*
Feyzabad **17**
fishing 15, *25*, **42**
floating market *27*
floods 26, 39, 41, *41*
    protection against *29*
Flores (island) **33**
Flores Sea **33**
food/food crops *4*, *16*, *20*
    Arabian peninsula *11*
    India *19*
    Indochina *28*, *29*
    Indonesia *33*
    Japan *25*
    Philippines *34*, *35*
forest products *34*, **42**
forests *see* rainforests
fruit *9*, *11*, *16*, *29*, 42, **42**
Fuji (mountain) *24*, *25*
Fukuoka **24**
Fukushima **25**
Fushun **21**
Fuzhou **21**

G
Gandhi, Mohandas *19*
Ganges River 18, **18–19**, **26**
gas, natural *6*, 31, 43, **43**
Gaza Strip **9**
Gaziantep **9**
gemstones *27*
General Santos **35**
George Town **30**

Georgia **4**, 5, 6, **6**
  statistics 6
Ghazni **17**
giant panda 20, 41
ginseng 23
glassware 16
Goa **18**
goats 16
Gobi Desert **21**
Godavari River **18**
Gorakhpur **19**
Gorgan **13**
Grand Canal **21**
Great Indian (Thar) Desert **18**
gross domestic product 43
  per capita 43
Guangzhou **21**
Guilin 20, **21**
Guiyang **21**
Gujranwala **17**
Gujrat **17**
Gulf, The 10, **11**, **12–13**
Guwahati **19**
Gwadar **16**
Gwalior **18**

H
Ha Giang **29**
Hachinohe **25**
Hadhramaut **11**
Hadur Shuayb (mountain) **11**
Haeju **22**
Hafar **11**
Haifa **9**
Haikou **21**
Hainan (island) **21**
Haiphong **29**
hajj 10
Hakakabo Razi (mountain) **27**
Hakodate **25**
Halla (mountain) **23**
Halmahera (island) **33**
Hamadan **12**
Hamamatsu **25**
Hamhung **23**
Han River **23**
Handan **21**
Hangzhou **21**
Hanoi **29**
Haora **19**
Haradh **11**
Harbin **21**
Harirud River **16**
'health' products 23
Hefei **21**
Hegang **21**
Helmand River **16-17**
Herat **16**
Hermon (mountain) **9**
high-tech industries **42**
hijab 10
Himalaya region 18, **18–19**, 19, 20
Hindu Kush **17**
Hinduism 4, 32, 36, 37, **37**
  gods, beliefs and practices 19
  temple 28
Hiroshima **24**
history 44–5, **45**
  great empires 44
Hitachi **25**
Ho Chi Minh 29
Ho Chi Minh City **29**
Hoa Binh **29**
Hokkaido (island) **25**
Homs **9**
Hong River **28–9**
Hong Kong 20, **21**, 21
Honshu (island) **24–5**
Hormuz, Strait of **11**, 13
Hotan **20**
housing:
  Indochina 29
  Indonesia 33
Huainan **21**
Huang He River **21**

Hue **29**
Hyderabad **17**, **18**
hydroelectricity **43**

I
Iloilo **35**
Imphal **19**
Inchon **22**
India **4–5**, 18-19, **18–19**
  religion 4, 19
  statistics 18
Indian Ocean **18–19**, **26–7**, 32
Indian subcontinent 18–19, **18–19**
  see also individual countries
Indigirka River **7**
Indochina 28, **28–9**
Indonesia **5**, 32, **32–3**
  capital 33
  statistics 32
Indore **18**
Indus River **17**, 17
Inland Sea **24**
Inthanon (mountain) **27**
Ipoh **30**
Iran **4**, 12, **12–13**
  economy 13
  statistics 12
Iraq **4**, 12, 12–13
  statistics 12
Irbil **12**
Irian Jaya see West Papua
Irkutsk **7**
iron ore 6
Irrawaddy River **26-7**
irrigation 15, 17
Irtysh River **6**, **15**
Iskenderun **9**
Islam 4, 13, 16, 32, 36, 37, **37**
  pilgrimage 10
  prayer 16
  women's clothes 10
Islamabad **17**
island numbers **32**, 36
Ismoili Somoni (mountain) **15**
Isparta **8**
Israel **4**, 8, **9**
  economy 9
  statistics 8
Istanbul **8**
Izmir **8**
Izmit 8, **8**

J
Jabal Ash Sham (mountain) **11**
Jabal Ramm (mountain) **9**
Jabal Yibir (mountain) **11**
Jaffna **19**
Jaipur **18**
Jakarta **32**, 36
Jalalabad **17**
Jammu **18**
Jamnagar **18**
Jamshedpur **19**
Japan **5**, 24–5, **24–5**
  capital 25
  religions 4
  statistics 24
Japan, Sea of 22, **23**, **24–5**
Java (island) **32**
Java Sea **32**
Jayapura **33**
jeepneys 35
Jehan, Shah 19
Jengish Chokusu **15**
Jerusalem 8, **9**, 36
Jews/Judaism 4, 8, 36, 37, **37**
Jhelum River **17**, **17**
Jiddah **10**
Jilin **21**
Jinan **21**
Jinzhou **21**
Jixi **21**
Jodhpur **18**
Johor Baharu **30**
Jolo (island) **34**

Jordan **4**, 8, **9**
  statistics 8
Jordan River **9**
Judaism see Jews
Jullundur **18**
jute 27

K
K2 (mountain) **17**
Kabul **17**
Kabul River **17**
Kaesong **22**
Kagoshima **24**
Kalimantan **32-3**
Kamchatka Peninsula 7, **7**
kampongs 33
Kanazawa **25**
Kanchenjunga (mountain) **19**
Kandahar **16**
Kangnung **23**
Kanpur **18**
Kaohsiung **21**
kapok 34
Kara Kum **14–15**
Kara Sea **7**
Karachi **17**
Karakorum Mountains **17**
Karbala **12**
Kars **9**
Kashan **13**
Kashi **20**
Kashmir **17**, **17**
Katmandu **19**
Kawasaki **25**
Kayseri **9**
Kazakhstan **4**, 5, 14, **14–15**
  space centre 15
  statistics 14
Kelang **30**
Keluang **30**
Kemerovo **7**
Kendari **33**
Keolradong (mountain) **20**
Kerman **13**
Khabarovsk **7**
Khabur River **9**
Khomeini, Ayatollah 13
Khon Kaen **27**
Khorramabad **12**
Khorramshahr **12**
Khulna **26**
Khyber Pass **17**
Kim Il Sung 22
  Jung Il 22
Kimchaek **23**
Kinabalu (mountain) **31**
Kiril Islands **7**
Kirkuk **12**
Kitakyushu **24**
Kizil River **9**
Kobe 25, **25**
Kochi **24**
Kolkata 18, **19**
Kolyma Mountains **7**
Kompong Cham **29**
Komsomolsk **7**
Konya **8**
Korean peninsula **5**, 22–3, **22–3**
Kota **18**
Kota Baharu **30**
Kota Kinabalu **31**
Kozhikode **18**
Kra, Isthmus of **27**
Krakatoa **32**, 33
Krasnoyarsk **7**
Kuala Belait **31**
Kuala Lumpur **5**
  Petronas Towers 5
Kuala Terengganu **30**
Kuantan **30**
Kuching **31**
Kudat **31**
Kugitangtau (mountain) **15**
Kula Kangri (mountain) **19**
Kumamoto **24**
Kunlun Mountains **20**
Kunming **21**

Kunsan **23**
Kupang (island) **33**
Kurdistan **9**, **12**
Kurds 12
Kurgan **6**
Kushiro **25**
Kuwait **4**, **12**, 12–13
  statistics 12
Kuwait (city) **12**
Kwangju **23**
Kyoto **25**
Kyrgyzstan **4**, **15**
  statistics 14
Kyushu (island) **24**
Kyzyl Kum **15**

L
Lahore **17**
Lalitpur **19**
land use 38
Lang Son **29**
Lanzhou **21**
Laoag **34**
Lao Cai **28**
Laos **5**, 28, **28–9**
  statistics 28
Laptev Sea **7**
Lashio **27**
Latakia **9**
leather goods 13
Lebanon **4**, 8, **9**
  statistics 8
Leh **18**
Lena River **7**
Leyte (island) **35**
Lhasa **20**
Linhai **21**
Liuzhou **21**
livestock **42**
  see also cattle; sheep
Lombok (island) **32**
Luang Prabang **28**
Lucknow **10**
Ludhiana **18**
Luoyang **21**
Luzon **34–5**

M
Macau 20, **21**
Madras see Chennai
Madurai **18**
Magadan **7**
mahoganies, Philippine 34
maize 34, **42**
Majene **33**
Malacca, Straits of **30**
Malang **32**
Malatya **9**
Malaysia 5, **5**, 30, **30–1**
  statistics 30
Maldives **4**, 18, **18**
  statistics 18
Male **18**
Manado **33**
Manama **11**
Mandalay **26**
Mangalore **18**
Manila **34**, 35
Manokwari **33**
manufacturing 5, 16, 28, 31, 34, **42**
Maoke Range **33**
Mao Zedong 20
Maras **9**
Marcos, Ferdinand 35
Mardan **17**
Marmara, Sea of **8**
Masan **23**
Masbate (island) **35**
Mashhad **13**
Matsue **24**
Matsuyama **24**
Mawlamyine **27**
Mayon Volcano **35**
Mazar-e-Sharif **17**
Mecca 10, **10**, 16
Medan **32**

Medina **10**
Mediterranean Asia 8–9, **8–9**
Mediterranean Sea **8–9**
Meerut **18**
Mekong River **20-1**, **28–9**, 29
Melaka **30**
Menderes River **8**
Mentawai Islands **32**
Mergui **27**
Meron (mountain) **9**
Mersin **9**
Mesopotamia 12, 44
metals/metal goods 6, 13, 27
military service 13
Mindanao (island) **35**
Mindoro (island) **34**
mining/minerals **42**
  Russia 6
Mirpur Khas **17**
Miyazaki **24**
Mocha **11**
Mohammed, Prophet 10, 44
Mohenjo Daro **17**
Mongolia **4–5**, 20, **20–1**
  nomads 21
  statistics 20
monkey-eating eagles 35
monsoons 39
Morioka **25**
Mosul **12**
motor cycles 25
Multan **17**
Mumbai (Bombay) **18**, 36
Mumtaz Mahal 19
Muscat **11**
Muslims see Islam
My Tho **29**
Myanmar **5**, 26, **26–7**
  statistics 26
Myitkyina **27**
Mymensingh **26**
Mysore **18**

N
Naga **35**
Nagasaki **24**
Nagoya **25**
Nagpur **18**
Nakhon Ratchasima **27**
Nakhon Sawan **27**
Nakhon Si Thammarat **27**
Namangan **15**
Nampo **22**
Nan River **27**
Nanchang **21**
Nanjing **21**
Narayanganj **26**
Narmada River **18**
Nawoly **15**
Negev Desert **9**
Negros (island) **35**
Nepal **4**, 18, **18–19**
  statistics 18
New Delhi **18**
New Guinea **33**
New Siberian Islands **7**
Nha Trang **29**
Nicosia **9**
Niigata **25**
Ningbo **21**
Ninh Binh **29**
Nordvik **7**
North Korea **5**, 22-3, **22–3**
  statistics 22
Novokuznetsk **7**
Novosibirsk **7**
Nowshak (mountain) **17**
Nukus **14**

O
oases 10, 39
Ob River **6**
oil industry **42**, 43
  Arabian peninsula 10, **11**
  Brunei and Malaysia 31
  Kuwait 13
  Russia and the Caucasus 6

Okayama **24**
Okhotsk **7**
Okhotsk, Sea of **7**
olive oil **42**
Olongapo **34**
Olympus (mountain) **9**
Oman **4**, 10, **11**
　statistics 10
Oman, Gulf of **11**
Omsk **6**
Oral **14**
orang-utans *32*, 41
Orsk **6**
oryx, Arabian *10*
Osaka **25**
Öskemen **15**
Osmaniye **9**

P
Pacific Ocean **24–5**, **34–5**
　see also 'ring of fire'
Padang **32**
Paektu (mountain) **23**
Pagadian **35**
Pakanbaru **32**
Pakistan **4**, 16–17, **16–17**
　economy 16
　statistics 16
Pakse **29**
Palawan (island) **34**
Palembang **32**
Palestine 8
palm oil *31*, 33
Palmyra **9**
Palu **33**
Pamirs (mountains) **15**
Panay **34–5**
panda *20*
Pathen **26**
Patna **19**
Pavlodar **15**
Persepolis 12, **13**
Peshawar **17**
Petra **9**, *9*
Petronas Towers *5*
Petropavl **15**
Petropavlosk-Kamchatskiy **7**
Philippines **5**, 34, **34–5**
　statistics 34
Phnom Penh **29**
phoshates 6
Phuket (island) **27**
Pidurutalagala (mountain) **19**
Ping River **27**
plants:
　Arabian peninsula *11*
　Bangladesh *27*
　endangered *41*
　Mediterranean Asia *9*
　see also rainforest
politics 44
　Communism 4, 6, 14, 20,
　　21, 22, 23, 28, 29, 44
pollution, environmental **40**,
　40–1
　Gulf War 13
Pontianak **32**
population 4, 5, **36**, 36–7
　China 20
　effect on environment **40**,
　　40–1
　India 18
pottery 13
poverty *5*, *35*, 44
Prome **26**
Puerto Princesa **34**
Puncak Jaya (mountain) **33**
Pune **18**
Punjab 17, **17**
Pusan **23**
Putao **27**
Pyongyang **22**

Q
Qaraghandy **15**
Qatar **4**, 10, **11**
　statistics 10

Qingdao **21**
Qiqihar **21**
Qom **13**
Qostanay **15**
Quang Tri **29**
Quetta **17**
Quezon City **34**
Qui Nhon **29**
Qurnat as Sawda (mountain) **9**

R
Rach Gia **29**
rainfall *39*, **39**
rainforest 32, *34*, **38**
　destruction of 32, 35, **40**,
　　40–1
Raipur **19**
Rajang River **31**
Rajkot **18**
Rajshahi **26**
Ranchi **19**
Rasht **12**
Ravi River 17, **17**
Rawalpindi **17**
Red Sea 10, **10**
religions *4*, *8*, *23*, 36, 37, **37**
religious conflict 6
Rey **13**
rhinoceros *41*
rice *4*, 19, *20*, 28, 31, *33*, 34,
　40, 42, **42**
　top producers 4
Rigestan Desert **16**
'ring of fire' 7, 24, 34, 41
Riyadh **11**
Roman Catholics *34*
Rub al Khali (Empty Quarter) **11**,
　11
rubber 31, 33, **42**
Russia and the Caucasus **4–5**,
　5, 6, **6–7**
　statistics 6

S
Sabah **31**
Saidpur **26**
Sakai **25**
Sakata **25**
Sakhalin (island) **7**
Salalah **11**
Salem **18**
Salween River **27**
Samar (island) **35**
Samarinda **32**
Samarkand **15**, *15*
Samsun **9**
San Pablo **34**
Sana **11**
Sandakan **31**
Sangihe Islands **33**
Sapporo **25**
Sarawak **31**
Sargodha **17**
Saudi Arabia **4**, 10, **10–11**
　economy 11
　statistics 10
Savannakhet **29**
Sayan Mountains **7**
Semarang **32**
Semey **15**
Sendai **25**
Seoul *22*, **23**, 36
Seremban **30**
Severnaya Zemlya (islands) **7**
Seyhan River **9**
Shanghai **21**, 36
Shantou **21**
Sharjah **11**
sheep 15, 16, **42**
Shenyang **21**
Shijiazhuang **21**
Shikarpur **17**
Shikoku (island) **24**
Shinto *4*
shipbuilding *21*, *23*, 25
'ships of the desert' *11*
Shiraz **13**

Shkhara (mountain) **6**
Sholapur **18**
Shymkent **15**
Sialkot **17**
Siamese cats *27*
Siargao (island) **35**
Siberia 6, **6–7**
Sibu **31**
silkworms *24*
Singapore **5**, *30*, **30**
　statistics 30
Singapore (city) **30**
Sintang **32**
Sinuiju **22**
Sisophon **28**
Sittwe **26**
Sivas **9**
slums *35*
Songkhla **27**
South China Sea **21**, **29**, **31**, **34**
South Korea **5**, 22-3, **22–3**
　capital 22
　economy 22, 23
　statistics 22
Southeast Asia **5**, 26
　see also individual countries
Soviet Union 6, 14
spices *33*, **42**
sports 24
Sri Lanka **4**, 18, **18–19**
　statistics 18
Srinagar **18**
Stalin, Joseph 6
Stanoyoy Range **7**
steppes 14
Stung Treng **29**
sugar cane 33, *35*
Sukkur **17**
Sulawesi (Celebes) island **33**
Sulu Sea **34**
Sumatra (island) **32**
Sumba (island) **33**
Sumbawa (island) **32**
Sumer/Sumerian people 4, 12
　temples *12*
sumo wrestling *24*
Surabaya **32**
Surakarta **32**
Surat **18**
Surat Thani **27**
Surgut **6**
Sutlej River 17, **17**
Syrdarya River **15**
Syria **4**, 8, **9**
　statistics 8
Syrian Desert **9**, **12**

T
Tabriz **12**
Tabuk **10**
Tacloban **35**
Taedong River **22**
Taegu **23**
Taejon **23**
Taipei **21**
Taiwan **5**, 20, **21**
　industry *21*
　statistics 20
Taiyuan **21**
Taiz **11**
Tajikistan **4**, **15**
　statistics 14
Taj Mahal *19*
Taklimakan Desert **20**
Taleban 16, 45
Talaud (islands) **33**
Tangshan **21**
Tanjungkarang **32**
tanks *13*
Taoism *4*
Tarlac **34**
Tarsus **9**
Tashkent **15**
Taurus Mountains **8–9**
Tawau **31**
Tawi-Tawi **34**
taxis *35*

Tay Ninh **29**
Tbilisi **6**
tea *19*, 33, **42**
Tehran *13*, **13**
Tel Aviv-Yafo **9**
temperatures *39*, **39**
Teneri (mountain) **15**
Thailand **5**, 26, **27**
　capital *27*
　statistics 26
Thailand, Gulf of **27**, **28–9**
Thimphu **19**
Thiruvananthapuram **18**
Thon Buri **27**
Three Gorges Dam **21**
Tian Shan (mountains) **20**
Tianjin **21**
Tibetan Plateau **20**
tigers *5*, 41
Tigris River **9**, 12, **12**
timber 31, 34
Timor *32*
Timur (Tamerlaine), Emperor 15
tin 27, *31*
Tiruchchirappalli **18**
Tirunelveli **18**
tobacco 34, **42**
Tokushima **24**
Tokyo **25**, *25*, 36
Tomsk **7**
Tonle Sap, Lake **28**
tourism *32*, **42**
Trabzon **9**
Trans-Siberian Railway *7*
Transcaucasia 6
Tripoli **9**
tropical storms 26, 41, **41**
Troy **8**
tsunami 18, 26, *27*, 33, 41, 45
Turkey **4**, 5, 8, **8–9**
　statistics 8
Turkmenbashi **14**
Turkmenistan **4**, **14–15**
　statistics 14
Tu Shan (mountain) **21**
Tuz, Lake **9**
Tyre **9**

U
Ubon Ratchathani **27**
Udon Thani **27**
Ujjain **18**
Ujung Pandang **33**
Ulan Bator **21**
Ulan Ude **7**
Ulsan **23**
United Arab Emirates **4**, 10, **11**
　statistics 10
Ur **12**, *12*
Ural Mountains 4, 6, **6**
Ural River 4, **6**, **14**
uranium 43
Urfa **9**
Urmia, Lake **12**
Ürümqi **20**
Uzbekistan **4**, **14–15**
　statistics 14

V
Vadodara **18**
Van **9**
Van, Lake **9**
Varanasi **19**
vegetation *38*, **38**
　Indonesia 32
　Philippines *34*
Verkhoyansk Range **7**
Vientiane **28**
Vietnam **5**, 28, **28–9**
　statistics 28

Vijayawada **19**
Vinh **29**
Vishakhapatnam **19**
Vladivostok **7**
volcanoes *7*, 24, *24*, **25**, 32,
　32, *33*, 34, **35**, 41, **41**

W
Waigeo (island) **33**
Wailing Wall *8*, *36*
Wakayama **25**
Wakkanai **25**
Warangai **18**
wars: 44–5
　Arab–Israeli 8
　ethnic conflicts 6, 12, 16,
　　17, 35
　Gulf 12, 13
　Iran–Iraq 12, 13
　Iraq 12, 13
　Korea 22, 23
　Vietnam 28
West Bank **9**
West Papua **33**
West Siberian Plain **6-7**
Western Ghats (mountains) **18**
Wetar (island) **33**
wheat 16, 19, **42**
wines **42**
Wonju **23**
Wonsan **23**
wool *see* sheep
woolly mammoths *6*
Wrangel Island **7**
writing:
　Japanese *25*
　Sumerian *4*
Wuhan **21**

X
Xi'an **21**
　terracotta army *44*
Xi Jiang River **21**

Y
Yablonovyy Range **7**
Yazd **13**
Yakutsk **7**
Yamagata **25**
Yanbu **10**
Yangon **26**
Yekaterinburg **6**
Yellow Sea **21**, 22, **22**
Yemen **4**, 10, **11**
　statistics 10
Yenisey River **7**
Yerevan **6**
Yining **20**
Yogyakarta **32**
Yokohama **25**
Yosu **23**
yurts *21*

Z
Zabid **11**
Zagros Mountains **12**
Zahedan **13**
Zamboanga **34**
Zanjan **12**
Zarqa **9**
Zaysan, Lake **15**
Zhambyl **15**
Zhaotong **21**
Zhengzhou **21**
Zhezqazghan **15**
Zibo **21**
ziggurats *12*
Zonguldak **8**

Picture credits
Photographs: David Scott 26, 42
The Hutchison Library 8, 13, 15, 17, 21, 22, 23, 34,
　35, 36